Stories of New Jersey

by
FRANK R. STOCKTON

with an Introduction by
MARY V. GAVER

RUTGERS UNIVERSITY PRESS
New Brunswick   New Jersey

Eighth Printing

Copyright © 1961 by Rutgers, The State University

Library of Congress Catalogue Number: 61-10267

SBN: 8135-0368-x Cloth Bound
SBN: 8135-0369-8 Paper Bound

Manufactured in the United States of America
by Quinn & Boden Company, Inc., Rahway, New Jersey

INTRODUCTION

The place of Frank R. Stockton in our literature is, according to his biographer, "in the second rank of those who were carrying the standard of American literary achievement during the last quarter of the nineteenth century." [1] Ranking not with Howells, or Clemens, or Henry James but rather with Aldrich, Eggleston, and Crawford, Stockton is known as an editor of *St. Nicholas Magazine,* as a prolific writer for the periodical press of his day, and as an author of one or two novels now read mainly by young people. His tour de force "The Lady, or The Tiger?", the hilarious novel *The Casting Away of Mrs. Lecks and Mrs. Aleshine,* and a handful of children's fanciful tales are the chief bases of his claim to our attention today. As an author of this rank, his work lives on in libraries, is enjoyed by discriminating readers, and is kept alive by publishers—as witness the 1955 reissue of his *Ting-a-Ling Tales* by Scribner's and the present reprint of his *Stories of New Jersey.*

Frank R. Stockton (1834-1902) was a member of a family closely connected with New Jersey history. De-

[1] Martin I. J. Griffin, *Frank R. Stockton: A Critical Biography* (Philadelphia: University of Pennsylvania Press, 1939), p. 144.

scended from a colonist who arrived on Long Island in 1656, one member of the family, Richard Stockton, was a signer of the Declaration of Independence, and another, Commodore Robert Stockton, is the subject of the last story in this volume. Frank R. Stockton, the author, lived most of his adult life in New Jersey, first in Nutley, then at Convent Station and at Morristown, before he moved to " Claymont " in West Virginia, just three years before his death. His memory is kept green in Nutley, where the public library has named the reading room for junior high school boys and girls in his honor and has decorated it with a mural by the artist Ivan Stoppe, who pictures the characters of Stockton's *Rudder Grange* against a background of rolling New Jersey countryside and winding river.

Although Stockton first worked as a wood engraver, he had written stories even as a high school student, and in 1870 his first collection of tales, *Ting-a-Ling,* was published. From then on he also wrote for the magazines, especially *Riverside, Hearth and Home,* and *St. Nicholas,* of which he became assistant editor when it was launched in 1873. In 1878, although he gave up his editorial work on *St. Nicholas* because of poor health, he continued to write for this famous magazine for children, and three of his best-known stories can now be read in *The St. Nicholas Anthology.*[2] Between 1899 and 1904, Scribner's issued a twenty-three-volume edition of Stockton's novels and stories.

Most of Stockton's stories for children are characterized by their imaginative, fanciful character and long episodic plots. His style gives free rein to a kind of absurd inventiveness and genteel humor, the narrative usually loose-knit

[2] Henry Steele Commager, ed., *The St. Nicholas Anthology* (2 vols., New York: Charles Scribner's Sons, 1948-1950).

iv

in construction. As one rereads the stories against the tradition of our present-day children's literature, however, only a few seem to be of the kind to appeal to the modern child. " The Griffin and the Minor Canon," inspired by his visit to Chester Cathedral, " The Bee-Man of Orn," a gentle satire on conformity, and " Old Pipes and the Dryad," which is tight-knit in construction and told with simplicity and real poetic quality—these seem to have permanent appeal, although they are at present in print only in anthologies.

In addition to a long line of fanciful tales of this kind, however, he wrote for young people two books of stories based on fact: *Stories of New Jersey* (1896) and *The Buccaneers and Pirates of Our Coasts* (1898). *Buccaneers and Pirates* was designed to be part of a Macmillan series of " Stories from American History " and was published serially in *St. Nicholas* before appearing in book form. In spite of the criticism of Stockton's biographer that it is an " antiseptic account " of a glamorous period in American history, the book has remained in print and is still read by boys interested in robust adventure stories.

Stories of New Jersey was also designed to be part of a series presenting the history of American states by famous writers, but only two other titles actually appeared: *Stories of Georgia* by Joel Chandler Harris and *Stories of Ohio* by William Dean Howells. Stockton signed the contract for the New Jersey volume on July 11, 1895, and it was published on May 25, 1896, in textbook format by the American Book Company; later in the year D. Appleton Company published a trade edition, using the same plates but a slightly different title, and it is from this edition that the present one has been reproduced. This reprint was initiated partly through the recommendation of a Morris

County librarian, Mrs. Mary Starin, just as Scribner's reissue of *Ting-a-Ling Tales* was stimulated by Mrs. Ogden Reid's continued enthusiasm for her childhood favorite. The persistent and lively readership of *Stories of New Jersey* is evidenced by the fact that the 1896 edition went through twenty-one printings, totaling over 100,000 copies, and did not actually go out of print until 1945.

That a book of local history limited to one of the smaller states, albeit historically an important one, had so long a life is probably due to the continuing appeal of Stockton's style, to the tenacity of librarians and historians who have kept his work alive in their collections, and to the interest of many readers in local history. For the reader of today the book has the appeal of a period piece. The stories are rambling, yet curiously effective. There is a kind of tongue-in-cheek humor, and the author's love for the woods, the rivers, and the people of New Jersey shines through every page. The illustrations are a potpourri of drawings by twenty-one different artists, characteristic of textbooks at the turn of the century. Although the different effects resulting from this mixture of techniques may seem odd to the reader accustomed to today's elaborately illustrated books, the Stockton illustrations do provide realistic detail in the nineteenth century manner. Among the illustrators were Dan Beard, C. Carleton, B. West Clinedinst, C. E. Hubbell, A. I. Keller, E. W. Kemble, M. F. Klepper, and Corwin K. Linson.

Stories of New Jersey has been reissued in facsimile at this time because it will help to meet the continuing demand for authentic and interestingly written information on New Jersey both for the adult reader and for the student. Although scholars have corrected certain historical inac-

vi

curacies, the Stockton stories are worthy of being kept alive, because of their basic soundness as well as because of their charm. The book provides at the same time an easy, readable introduction to New Jersey history, chronologically arranged to present an over-all picture of the state's early development through the Mexican War period. Some other books, excellent as they are, deal with special phases or periods, are rambling memoirs in form, or are too general to give the details of some of the stories found in Stockton. Here the reader will find not only an account of the wild animals and the Indian tribes during colonial times but also one of the few coherent accounts of the patriot spy John Honeyman. Naval heroes, privateersmen like Captain Huddy, schoolmasters and doctors, women like Tempe Wick and Penelope Stout, inventors like John Fitch, and military leaders like Lord Stirling and, of course, General Washington, all have their day in this storehouse of New Jersey history. The list of " Authorities " in Stockton's Table of Contents may be used as a comprehensive guide to the standard works on the state up to his time. Major current works of Jerseyana are listed in " A Basic Library of New Jersey History," added in this edition.

May this edition of a book long heavily used and highly valued in libraries give a new generation of students and readers a panoramic view of the history of a proud state and a new appreciation of an author who would have been glad to be known as a " professional storyteller."

MARY V. GAVER
Professor of Library Service
Rutgers, The State University
New Brunswick, New Jersey

vii

PREFACE.

THIS volume of stories, composed of historical incidents, or material connected with the history of New Jersey, is not intended to be a record, even in a condensed form, of the rise and progress of the State. The stories are arranged chronologically, but there has been no attempt to give a complete and continuous account of events or epochs. The material for the stories has been collected from many sources; and the selections have been made with regard to the interest, the instructiveness, and as far as possible the novelty, of the matter chosen. There has been a constant endeavor, however, to present a series of historical incidents in a panoramic form, so that the reading of the stories in their regular succession would give an impressive idea of the discovery and settlement of the State, of its people, manners, and customs, and of its progress and achievements, as it was gradually evolved from the Indian region of Scheyichbi into the State of New Jersey.

In these stories there is nothing imaginative or fanciful, except where a reference is made to the early

I

imaginings and fancies of the aborigines. The stories are not founded on facts, but they are made up of facts carefully collected from the authorities referred to in the table of contents. Some of the stories are well known, but could not be omitted because of their representative character; but others, it is hoped, will be found familiar only to the professed student of history. The period of the stories extends from the earliest times of Indian tradition down to what may be called our own day; but as there was so much available matter, and so little space for it, and as there was no intention to give a comprehensive history of the State, it was deemed well to deal only with the incidents and people that have passed out of the boundaries of current history.

CONTENTS.

———◆◦◆———

3

Stories of New Jersey

STORIES OF NEW JERSEY.

THE STORY OF THE DISCOVERY OF SCHEYICHBI.

THE North American Indians, the earliest inhabitants of this country of whom we know anything
definite, were great story-tellers; and their histories
consist entirely of stories handed down from parents
to children, or, more likely, from grandparents to
grandchildren, for grandfathers and grandmothers are

generally more willing to tell stories than fathers or mothers. And so these traditions, probably a good deal brightened by being passed along century after century, came down to the Indians who were first met by white people, and thus we have heard many of them.

The stories told by the Indians inhabiting the country which is now the Middle States, all agree that their remote forefathers came from some region beyond the Mississippi River. Like the traditions of most nations, these go so very far back that they are vague and misty; but, as this gave the Indians a great opportunity for their imaginations, it is not wonderful that they improved it. These Indians believed that in the very earliest stages of their existence they were all animals, and lived in caves under the earth. They were hunters; but their game consisted of mice, and creatures of that sort. One of them accidentally discovered a hole by which he got out on the surface of the ground; and, finding it so exceedingly pleasant, it was not long before the whole of his tribe came out, and began life in the light of day.

It may be supposed that these animals gradually changed to human beings, and built villages, and planted corn; but in one respect they did not change, nor have they changed at this present day. Many of them still call themselves after the names of animals; and now the greater part of the noted Indians of our country have such names as "Sitting Bull," "Black Bear," and "Red Horse." But the stories say that all of the animals did not come out of their underground homes. Among these were the hedgehog and the rabbit; and so some of the tribes will not eat these animals, because in so doing they may be eating their family connections.

Gradually the ancestors of the Indians who told their stories to the first settlers, and who afterwards called themselves the Lenni-Lenape, moved eastward, and after many years they reached the Mississippi River. By this time they had become a powerful body. But in the course of their journeys they discovered that they were not the earliest emigrants in this direction, for they met with a great tribe called the Mengwe, later known as the Iroquois, who had come from a country west of the Mississippi, but farther north than that of our Indians.

We do not hear that these two great tribes of early Indians interfered with each other; but when the Lenni-Lenape investigated the other side of the Mississippi, they found there still another nation, powerful, numerous, and warlike. These were called the Alligewi, from which we have derived the name Allegheny. At first the latter tribe was inclined to allow the Lenape to pass the river; but after a time, finding that the newcomers were so numerous, they fell upon them and drove them back.

But the Indians at that remote period must have been as doggedly determined to move eastward as are our pioneers to move westward; and they were not to be stopped by rivers, mountains, or savage enemies. The Lenape were not strong enough to fight the Alligewi by themselves, and so they formed an alli-

ance with the Mengwe; and these two nations together made war upon the Alligewi, and in the course
of time overcame them, and drove them entirely from
their country.

After years, or perhaps centuries (for there are no
definite statements of time in these Indian traditions),
the Mengwe and the Lenape, who had been living
together in the country of the Alligewi, separated;
and the Mengwe emigrated to the lands near the
Great Lakes, while the Lenape slowly continued their
progress eastward.

They crossed the Alleghanies, and discovered a
great river, which they called Susquehanna, and then
they moved on until they came to the Delaware.
This grand stream pleased them so much, that they
gave it a name of honor, and called it the Lenape-
wihittuck, or "The River of the Lenape." Then they
crossed the river and discovered New Jersey.

Here they found a pleasant climate, plenty of
game, and no human inhabitants whatever. They
therefore appropriated it as their own, and gave it
the name of Scheyichbi; and any one who endeav-
ors to pronounce this name will be likely to feel
glad that it was afterwards changed by the white
settlers.

Before this first discovery of New Jersey, the Lenni-
Lenape had settled themselves in the beautiful and
fertile country about the Susquehanna and the west
shore of the Delaware, and here established their
right to their name, which signifies "original people;"
and if their stories are correct, they certainly are the

original inhabitants of this region, and they discovered New Jersey from the west, and took rightful possession of it.

It is a law of nations, founded then upon the same principles of justice as it stands upon now, that discovery by a nation, or the agent of a nation, of unknown lands entirely uninhabited, gives the discoverers the right to those lands; and, in accordance with that law, the Lenape became the discoverers and original owners of New Jersey.

We will not now allude to the rights they then acquired to the country which is now Pennsylvania and other States, because we are confining ourselves to what relates to the country of Scheyichbi, the land where their eastward migrations ceased. Now, they could go no farther towards the rising sun, and they were satisfied to stop.

These Lenape, or "Grandfather Tribe" as they were often called, were not merely cruel and ignorant savages: they had many admirable traits of character, and some of their manners and customs might well have been imitated by those who found them here.

They had an admirable system of government; and at regularly appointed periods their wisest men met at the great "Council House" to make laws, and arrange the affairs of the nation. Their conduct in their councils was far more decorous and becoming than that we often hear of among legislators of the present day, whether they are met together in Congress, Parliament, or Reichstag. These chiefs, chosen for their wisdom and experience, treated each other with the

highest regard and respect. When one of them arose
to address his fellow-legislators, every man in the
council room paid the strictest attention to what he
said; and interruptions, jeers, and ridicule, such as
legislators often make use of at the present day, were
totally unknown among these grave and earnest
Indians.

There can be no doubt that the Lenape were superior to other Indian nations, and worthy of the proud
title which they gave themselves; and in later years,
when the river was named after Lord De la Warre,
and they were called the Delawares, they were considered the noblest of the Indian tribes.

I dwell upon the good qualities and high character
of the Lenape, because it was from their main body
that numerous tribes came across the Delaware River,
and became the first Jerseymen, or, if any one likes
it better, Scheyichbians. They settled in many pleasant places, building wigwam villages, many of which
have since grown into modern towns, and still bear
their old Indian names. In fact, the modern Jerseyman has had the good sense to preserve a great many
of the names given to rivers, mountains, and villages
by the first owners of the soil.

But, after all, Scheyichbi was not sufficiently discovered and settled for the purposes of civilization,
and its fertile soil waited long for the footsteps of the
new immigrants. These came at last from the east.

About the end of the fifteenth century there was
a strong desire among the maritime nations of Europe
to find a short passage to China and the East Indies.

It was for that reason that Columbus set out on his expedition; but with his story we have nothing to do, for he did not discover the continent of North America, and in fact never saw it. But after John Cabot and his son Sebastian, then looking for a passage to Cathay in the interest of the King of England, made a voyage to North America, and had contented themselves with discovering New-foundland, Sebastian came back again, and accomplished a great deal more. He sailed along the coast from Labrador to the southern end of Florida, and in the course of this voyage discovered New Jersey. He made a map of the whole coast, and claimed all the country back of it for the King of England.

There is no proof that Cabot knew whether this country had inhabitants or not. He saw it from his ships; but he did not make any attempt to settle it, and thus establish a legal right to the soil. He simply declared it the property of the Crown of England, and it is upon this claim that England afterward based her right to the eastern coast of North America.

And so New Jersey was discovered from the east.

About a quarter of a century after Sebastian Cabot's voyage, the French took up the idea that they would like to discover something, and Francis I. sent an Italian mariner, named John Verrazano, across the Atlantic Ocean.

After having sailed far enough, John Verrazano discovered the coast of North America, which he called "a new land never before seen by any man, ancient or modern." He took possession of it in the name of his king, and, in order to settle the matter, called the whole coast New France. There is reason to believe that Verrazano discovered the southern part of New Jersey, for in sailing northward he probably entered Delaware Bay.

But it appears that New Jersey was not yet sufficiently discovered, and after having been left for a long time in the possession of its true owners, the Lenni-Lenape, it was again visited by Europeans. In 1609 the celebrated Henry Hudson, then in the service of the Dutch East India Company, started westward to try to find a northwest passage to China. In those bygone days, whenever a European explorer set out to find an easy passage to the East, he was very apt to discover New Jersey; and this is what happened to Henry Hudson. He first discovered it on the south, and partially explored Delaware Bay; then he sailed up the coast and entered New York Bay, and sailed some distance up the river which now bears his name.

Hudson did more for New Jersey than any of the other discoverers, for his men were the first Europeans

who ever set foot upon its soil. Some of them landed
in the vicinity of Bergen Point, and were met in a
friendly way by a great many of the original inhabitants. But the fact that he found here possessors of
the soil made no difference to Hudson: he claimed the
country for the Dutch. Five years afterwards, that
nation made a settlement at New York, and claiming
the whole of the surrounding country, including New
Jersey, gave it the name of New Netherland.

Thus was New Jersey discovered on the north; and
after the efforts of four nations, — the Indians first,
the English under Cabot, the French, and the Dutch
(for Hudson was now in the service of that nation), —
it may be said to have been entirely discovered.

THE STORY OF A PEACEMAKER.

AFTER the outside boundaries of New Jersey had been pretty thoroughly discovered, it was quite natural that some nations who laid claim to the State should desire to find out something in regard to its interior, and make settlements upon its soil.

This was not done by the English, who had made the first claim to the land, but by the Dutch. In the early part of the seventeenth century, the West India Company of Holland sent out a ship containing the foundation for a little colony, — men, provisions, and all things necessary. They sailed into Delaware Bay; and the commander, Cornelius Jacobsen Mey, gave his name to Cape May. The expedition went up the Delaware River till they reached Timber Creek, probably not much more than ten miles from the spot where Philadelphia now stands. There they settled, and built a fort, which they called Fort Nassau. But this was not looked upon with favor by the Indians, and it was not long before the whole colony was destroyed.

This unfortunate beginning of the white settlement of New Jersey did not deter the Dutch, who are a persevering and dogged people. About twelve years later, another Dutch commander, De Vries, sailed up the

Delaware River, or, as the Dutch called it, the South River; his main object being to catch whales, very different from the Delaware fisheries of the present day. He set up a little colony on shore; but it appears that the Indians were very much opposed to this sort of thing, and this settlement was destroyed before long.

But De Vries still kept up the whaling business; and in the course of time, getting out of provisions, he left his vessel, and sailed up the river in a small craft which was called the "Squirrel." He went up as far as the deserted Fort Nassau, and there anchored to trade with the Indians.

It is quite plain that the Indians of New Jersey were now greatly concerned about the visits of white people to their shore; for they perceived

Indian Rattle.

that these newcomers were inclined to settle and occupy such places as pleased their fancy, without asking permission, or proposing to buy or to pay rent. All this was very disagreeable to the red men, who had never shown any disposition to open up their country to foreign immigration.

When De Vries anchored, he was very well received; and about forty Indians came on board his yacht, and made a call upon him. They were dressed in their best, and, in order to make the visit more agreeable, they brought some of their musical instruments with them, and gave the Dutchmen a taste of Indian music.

Indian Flute.

The dress of some of these visitors was a surprise to De Vries and his men, of whom there were only seven on the yacht. It was winter time, and most of the Indians were arrayed in furs, but several of them wore jackets made in the English fashion. The visitors were very friendly, and urged De Vries to sail his vessel up a stream, now known as Big Timber Creek, which, they declared, was a much better place for trading.

Now, according to some of the old histories, a woman appeared in the double character of peacemaker and guardian angel.

Indian Tam-tam.

Among the Lenni-Lenape, as well as the other tribes of North America, women often had a peculiar part to play in national and social affairs. If ever the services of a peacemaker were desired, that position was always given to a woman. It was considered derogatory to the dignity of a male Indian that he should at any time, of his own accord, desire peace. He and his enemy might both be thoroughly tired of fighting; but neither of them would lower himself in his own estimation, and in the estimation of his countrymen, by allowing any man to know the state of his mind.

But he did not in the least object to tell his wife that he wanted to stop fighting; and she, very gladly in most cases, would confer with the wife of the other brave; and when they had concluded peace, the two men would immediately sit down together, smoke the calumet, and be good friends; and all this without the slightest loss of dignity.

This method of making peace was pursued not only by individuals, but by nations. Very often women had this important political duty thrust upon them, — a duty for which they were probably very well qualified, for it is seldom that the women of a nation desire war.

This national disposition in regard to peacemaking was once the occasion of a serious misfortune to the tribe of Lenni-Lenape. The tribes to the north, who had formed themselves into a powerful body called the Five Nations, had long been jealous of their neighbors the Lenni-Lenape, and contrived a plan to humiliate them, and render them less important in the eyes of the Indian world. Being at war with some other tribes, these Five Nations came to the Lenni-Lenape and pretended to desire peace, but stated that this was too important a case to be managed by women. They declared that this was a great work, which should be given only into the hands of a quiet, dignified, and honorable tribe, such as their great neighbors, and urged the Lenape to undertake negotiations for the cessation of hostilities.

As all this seemed reasonable enough, the Lenape were at last persuaded to become peacemakers, and, as might be supposed, they were entirely successful; but they suffered for their kindness and good feeling. Ever afterwards they were looked upon by other Indian tribes as no better than women. In Cooper's novels there are references to the fact that the noble Lenape were sneered at as peacemakers and squaws.

But we will now return to our guardian angel. It was after a visit of the Indians to the vessel of De

Vries, that the peacemaking instinct took possession of the wife of one of the Indian chiefs; and quietly and stealthily, unperceived by her people, she managed to get on board the "Squirrel," when she informed the commander of the real object of his visitors, who had invited him to sail up Timber Creek. It was the desire of the Indians to destroy this company of white men; and the narrow stream where they wished to make the attempt was much better adapted for their purpose than the broad waters of the river.

Wishing to prevent an encounter in which the sturdy Dutchmen would probably kill some of her countrymen before they themselves were destroyed, she had come to implore the whites not to run into the trap which had been set for them. She told them that the crew of an English shallop, which not long before had come to visit the place, probably from a ship afraid to venture higher up the river, had all been slaughtered, and that it was the jackets of these men that some of her countrymen were wearing.

Like a sensible man, De Vries paid attention to this story, and did not venture into Timber Creek. Whether or not he rewarded the good woman who came to warn him of his danger, is not known; but his account of the affair places her in the position of one worthy of a monument by the women of the State.

When the Indians came again to De Vries, he declared to them that his Great Spirit, or "Maneto," had revealed their wicked purposes, and that he would not sail up the Timber Creek, nor would he allow one of them upon his vessel; and, having ordered them all on shore, he dropped some distance down the river.

This conduct doubtless inspired the Indians with great respect for the brave Dutchmen, and shortly afterwards the chiefs from nine different tribes came on board the "Squirrel" for the purpose of making a treaty of peace and commerce with the Dutch. All of these were now dressed in furs, which were their ordinary garments; but some of them were recognized as the same men who had formerly worn the jackets of the murdered English sailors. These, however, were just as cordial and friendly as any of the others, and there is no reason to suppose that they now intended treachery. The visitors sat down on the deck of the yacht, and held a regular council, and, with appropriate ceremonies, made presents of beaver skins to the whites, and solemnly concluded a treaty of friendship.

THE WINNING OF THE PRIZE.

AFTER the importance of the discovery of North America came to be properly appreciated by the nations of Europe, the ownership was looked upon as a great national prize, and there were several nations who were anxious to play for it. This country, so readily approached by the Delaware, became attractive not only to kings and sovereigns, but to settlers and immigrants. Gustavus Adolphus of Sweden granted a charter to a company called the West India Company, which was formed for the purpose of making settlements on the shores of the Delaware Bay and River, and commissioned them to take possession of this country, without the slightest regard to what the English sovereign and the Dutch sovereign had granted to their subjects.

The Swedes came to Delaware Bay. They stopped for a while at Cape Henlopen; and then, of course, they sailed up the Delaware, when things soon began to be very disagreeable between themselves and the Dutch, who were there before them.

The Swedes were a warlike set of people, and they held their ground very well. Besides making some settlements, they built a fort which they called Elsin-

burgh; and, if a Dutch ship happened to pass by
that fort, it was obliged to strike its flag in token of
submission to a superior power. The Indians, who
were perhaps as much opposed to the Swedish settlement as they had been to those
of other nations, do not
appear to have been able
to attack this fort with
any success; and as
for the Dutch, it is
not certain that they
even attempted it. So
the Swedes at that
time governed the
passage up and down
the Delaware, as the
English now govern
the passage through
the Straits of Gibraltar.

It was probably win-
ter time or cool weather
when the Swedes built
their proud fort on the banks
of that river which they now
named "New Swedeland Stream;"
but when the warm and pleasant days came on, and it
was easy to travel from the interior to the river shore,
and when the weather was so mild that it was quite
possible to spend the nights in the woods without injury,
there came an enemy to Fort Elsinburgh which proved
far more formidable than the Indians or Dutch.

The fort was surrounded; and frequent and violent attacks were made upon it, especially in the night, when it was almost impossible for the garrison to defend themselves. Many bloody single combats took place in which the enemy generally fell, for in bodily prowess a Swede was always superior to any one of the attacking force. But no matter how many assailants were killed, the main body seemed as powerful and determined as ever. In course of time the valiant Swedes were obliged to give way before their enemy. They struck their flag, evacuated the fort, and departed entirely from the place where they had hoped a flourishing settlement would spring up under the protection of their fort.

The enemy which attacked and routed the Swedes was a large and invincible army of mosquitoes, against whom their guns, their pistols, their swords, their spears, and their ramparts afforded them no defense. After that, the deserted fort was known as Mygenborg, meaning Mosquito Fort.

The Dutch looked with great disfavor on the Swedes, who continued to establish themselves at various points; and although they did not make an alliance with the body of natives who had driven these northern people away from Elsinburgh, — for a compact of that kind would be dangerous in many ways, — they took up the matter by themselves; and finally the Dutch.

under their valiant Peter Stuyvesant, completely conquered the Swedes, and sent their leaders to Holland, while the ordinary settlers submitted to the Dutch.

But this state of things did not continue very long; for the English, who, although they had not yet settled in New Jersey, had never given up their pretensions as the original discoverers, came in strong force, subdued the Dutch, occupied their principal town, New Amsterdam, and took possession of the country, including New Jersey.

But it seemed to be a good deal easier to discover New Jersey than finally to settle its ownership. Now that the Dutch and the Swedes were disposed of, there arose difficulties regarding the English claims to the State. Early in the seventeenth century, Queen Elizabeth had granted an immense tract of land to Sir Walter Raleigh, which was called Virginia, and that included the whole of New Jersey. Afterwards Charles II. granted to his brother, the Duke of York, an immense tract of land, which also included New Jersey, and which was called New York. So what is now New Jersey was then at the same time both Virginia and New York.

The Duke of York, who then owned New Jersey, leased the whole State — lands, forests, rivers, wigwams, Indians, fisheries, Dutch settlers, Swedish settlers, everything — to John Berkeley (Baron of Stratton) and Sir George Carteret for the sum of twenty nobles per year (thirty-two dollars of our money). Some authorities, indeed, state that the sum paid was much smaller.

After a time, however, the claims of Virginia were withdrawn; and not only did Berkeley and Carteret enjoy undisturbed possession of the State, but they gave it a name, and called it *Nova Cæsaria*, or New Jersey, its name being given on account of Carteret's connection with the Isle of Jersey. The Latin name was used for a time; but the settlers preferred English, and so the name now stands. New Jersey was soon afterwards divided into two provinces, — East Jersey and West Jersey. The accompanying map shows the line of division between the two provinces, which was made in 1676. It ran from the southern end of what is now Long Beach, in Little Egg Harbor, to a point on the Delaware River. Two other lines of partition were afterwards made, both starting from the same point on the seacoast; one running somewhat to the west, and the other to the east, of the original line.

After some changes in the proprietorship of the Colony, West Jersey came into the possession of twelve men, one of whom was the celebrated William Penn, whose connection with West Jersey began six years before he had anything to do with Pennsylvania.

Penn and his colleagues gave West Jersey a purely democratic government, founded upon principles of justice and charity, in which the people themselves ruled. Full freedom in regard to religious views was insured; trial by jury was granted; and punishments were made as lenient as possible, with a view to the prevention of crimes rather than the infliction of penalties. The result of this was that for a long time

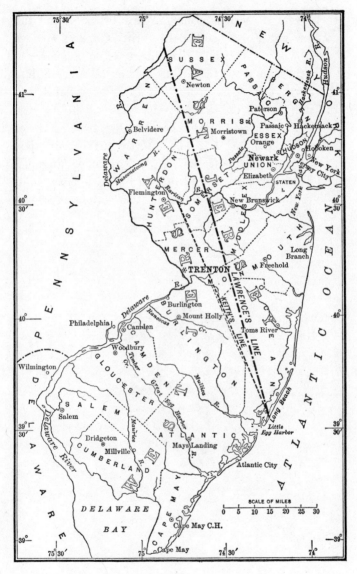

there were no serious crimes in this Province, and the country was rapidly settled by thrifty Quakers anxious to live where they would have liberty of conscience.

In the course of time, East Jersey also came into the possession of Penn and his eleven associates, and the number of proprietors was increased to twenty-four. At the end of the century the two provinces were united into one, and shortly afterwards they passed into the possession of the Crown of England, and became subject to the ordinary British laws. For a long time afterwards, however, the State was known as the "Jerseys."

HOW SCHEYICHBI REALLY BECAME NEW JERSEY.

A POINT in the history of New Jersey, more important in a moral point of view than that of its European ownership, was that of the purchase of the lands from the first and true owners, the Indians. As has been said, Berkeley and Carteret issued an injunction that the settlers should purchase their lands from the tribes which had lived upon them. This system was subsequently carried out until every foot of the land of the whole State was bought and paid for, — the first transactions of the kind, having taken place several years before Penn's treaty with the Indians in Pennsylvania.

Up to the time when the country finally passed into the hands of the English, the Indians had resisted the attempts of the whites to settle among them; but now, finding that they were to be fairly dealt with, a better feeling arose, and the red men were content to dwell with the whites as friends and neighbors. Of course, all the settlers did not promptly pay for their lands, and there were some minor disputes from this cause; but in general the whites regularly purchased the land upon which they intended to make their homes, and in time all were obliged to do so. As may be supposed, very large prices were not paid for these lands; but the transactions were strictly honorable, because the parties on each side gave what they had, and all were satisfied with what they got.

The payments for land frequently consisted partly of ready-made coats, kettles, and in some cases of jew's-harps. Tracts of land large enough for a town were sometimes sold for a barrel of cider. Now, this might appear rather a hard bargain for the Indians; but it must be considered that they had more land than they wanted, and no ready-made coats, or kettles, or jew's-harps, or cider.

But it was not to be expected that the Indians would always be satisfied with their treatment; and in fact they had a good many grievances. As has

been said, a settler sometimes established himself on
a good piece of land without consulting the Indians
of the neighborhood, or offering them payment, and
in such cases there would be remonstrances from the
red men. Then, again, the whites could not always
understand the nature of Indian bargains. A man
would buy a piece of land, and think that he owned
not only the ground, but all that grew upon it, all
that flew in the air above it, and everything that
swam in its waters; and when the Indians, after
having received payment for the farm, came there
to hunt and fish, and strip the bark off the trees,
the purchaser was apt to object.

A notable difficulty of this kind occurred on Sandy
Hook, where a man named Hartshorne had bought a
tract of land from the Indians, and afterwards found,
that, according to their ideas, he had no exclusive
right to the fish, game, and timber of his new purchase; and he was especially made to understand
that he had not bought the wild plums. This matter
of the ownership of the plums afterwards became a
source of considerable trouble, and was settled by
Hartshorne paying to the chief of the neighboring
tribe the sum of thirteen shillings, by which he acquired the entire right to the plums and all the other
things on his land.

The Indians had also a grievance of a different
kind. There was a conference held in Burlington,
between the Indians and the whites, in 1678, which
was convened on account of a complaint by the Indians that the English, in selling them some ready-

made coats, had also sold them the smallpox. The temper of the Indians may be shown by one of their speeches on this occasion. A leading chief declared: "We are willing to have a broad path for you and us to walk in; and if an Indian is asleep in this path, the Englishman shall pass by him and do him no harm; and if an Englishman is asleep in the path, the Indian shall pass him by and say, 'He is an Englishman; he is asleep; let him alone; he loves to sleep!' It shall be a plain path. There must not be in this path a stump to hurt our feet. And as for the smallpox, it was once in my grandfather's time, and it could not be the English that could send it to us then, there being no English in the country. And it was once in my father's time, they could not send it to us then, neither. And now it is in my time, I do not believe that they have sent it to us now. I do believe it is the man above who has sent it to us." Soon after this, the two parties exchanged presents, and went away satisfied.

For many years after this, there seem to have been few or no troubles between the Indians and the settlers of New Jersey. But matters changed about the middle of the next century; and when the Indian wars began in Pennsylvania, the red men of New Jersey showed symptoms of hostility to the whites. Matters grew worse and worse; and the Indians began to murder families, burn buildings, and carry away prisoners.

This state of affairs grew so alarming that the Legislature took the matter in hand. They appointed commissioners to examine into the treatment of the Indians, and see if there were any good cause for their sudden enmity; and, after a conference with some of the chiefs, a bill was passed by the Legislature to put an end to a good many of the impositions of which the Indians complained. Among these was a habit of the whites of giving the Indians spirits, and then making bargains with them when they were not at all in a condition to do business of that kind. The Indians also complained of the practice of trapping deer, thus decreasing the game in the forests, and the occupation of land, without payment, by the settlers who were continually coming into the country.

Another bill was passed appropriating £1600 to buy from the Indians the entire right to all the lands which they yet held in New Jersey. But as there was no desire to banish the Indians from their native land, one half of this sum was reserved as payment for a large tract of land, or reservation, which should be their home, and on which no white man would have any right to settle, whether he was willing to buy the land or not. When this had been done, it was necessary to submit the matter to the Indians; and a council was called at Burlington, at which were present the governor of the Province, and some of the most prominent Indian chiefs.

At this conference there was a notable exhibition of Indian etiquette. The governor had called the Minisinks, a tribe of the Delawares, to meet him; and they had informed the Mingoians, who, with some other northern tribes, were then gathered together at the grand council fire at the forks of the Delaware, where is now Easton. This was done, because at that time the Mingoians considered themselves superior to the Delawares, from whom proper respect was due.

One of the chiefs from the council fire was sent down to represent the Mingoians. After some speeches were made, he told the white governor that the Mini-sinks, being Delawares, were women, and were not able of themselves to make treaties, therefore he had come down to look into the matter. As his people were then holding a grand council fire at the forks of the Delaware, they did not wish to put it out and build another council fire on this side of the Delaware. The reason which he gave for this was figurative and Indian-like.

He stated that the river roared and thundered, and made a great deal of noise; and, if the council were held on this side, the distant Indian nations who dwelt to the west of the Delaware could not hear what was said at the council, and therefore it would be unfair to them to hold it on this side of the river. He con-cluded with a cordial invitation to the governor and his party to meet the Indians at their own council fire.

About a month afterward, the governor, with some members of the Legislature, and other white people from New Jersey and Pennsylvania, met over five hundred Indians at the forks of the Delaware in grand council. Some of the speeches on this occasion were very interesting. A chief of the United Nations, speaking for the Delawares, who, having made them-selves women by becoming peacemakers, had no right to speak for themselves, addressed the council as follows : —

"Brethren, we now remove the hatchet out of your heads, that was struck into it by our cousins the Delawares. It was a French hatchet they unfortunately made use of, by the instigation of the French. We take it out of your heads, and bury it underground, where it shall always rest, and never be taken up again. Our cousins the Delawares have assured us they will never think of war against their brethren the English any more, but will employ their thoughts about peace and cultivating friendship with them, and never suffer enmity against them to enter into their minds again."

Another chief said : "Brethren, I speak in behalf of the younger nations, — those who are confederated with the Six Nations, the Cayugas, Oneidas, Tuscaroras, Tutaloes, Nanticokes, and Conoys. A road has been made from our country to this council fire, that we might treat about friendship ; and as we came down the road, we saw, that, by some misfortune or other, blood has lately been spilt on it. Now, we make the road wider and clearer. We take the blood away out of it, and likewise out of the council chamber, which may have been stained. We wash it all away, and desire it may not be seen any more, and we take the hatchet out of your heads."

The governor of New Jersey also addressed this council, particularly urging them to require the Indians who had taken away prisoners to return these unfortunate people to their homes. In answer to this, one of the great chiefs of the United Nations made a speech to the Minisinks and the Delawares, in which he gave them a good scolding for not having returned these prisoners before; for it seemed that they had promised to do so.

The council continued several days; and the Minisinks promised faithfully that they would search all the towns in their territory for prisoners, and return them to their own people. This matter having been settled, Governor Bernard made a formal proposition to buy all the lands which the Indians still retained in New Jersey; and, after a good deal of consultation, the chiefs of the United Nations advised the Minisinks and Delawares to accept the terms which were offered. After much talk, it was done, the necessary papers were signed, and the State of New Jersey was formally bought from its Indian owners.

After this great matter had been settled, the tract of land which was to be set apart for the occupation of the Indians of the State, south of the Raritan River, in Burlington County, was purchased. It consisted of three thousand acres, which reached to the seacoast. There was plenty of fishing on it, and there were wild lands and forests, in which game abounded. Here the Indians could live as they pleased after their old-fashioned fashions, and never need fear disturbance by white men. Here they removed, and here they did live, apparently perfectly satisfied; and after this there were no further Indian troubles in New Jersey.

The Indians on this reservation came to be known as the Edge-Pillocks, and in course of time considerable civilization crept in among them. It is a proof

of this, that one of them, who took the name of Stephen
Calvin, kept a school, and that his son Bartholomew
went to Princeton College, and afterwards taught
school. It is said that in his school there were as
many white scholars as Indians.

In 1801 these Edge-Pillock Indians were invited by
the Mohicans of New York to leave their New Jersey home and come and live with them. In their
invitation the Mohicans said they would like them
"to pack up your mat and come and eat out of our
dish, which is large enough for all, and our necks are
stretched in looking toward the fireside of our grandfather till they are as long as cranes."

The Edge-Pillocks sold their reservation, had the
money invested for them in United States stocks, and
went to join the Mohicans. After that, both tribes decided to buy land in Michigan, and the Edge-Pillocks
disposed of their stocks to pay for their share.

But our New Jersey Indians did not fare well in
the West. Their fortunes did not prosper, and they
grew poorer and poorer, until in 1832 their numbers
decreased to about forty. Feeling the pressure of
poverty, their Indian disposition suggested to them a
remedy. They remembered, that, although they had
sold their reservation, nothing had been said in the
deeds concerning the game and the fish on the property; and they chose to consider that these still belonged to them. They therefore sent Bartholomew
Calvin, who was now their oldest chief, to New Jersey
to ask the Legislature to buy these remaining rights.
The Legislature promptly agreed to do this, and ap-

propriated two thousand dollars, which was the sum Bartholomew named, to buy of the Indians all their remaining rights of every kind in New Jersey.

This act may be considered as one of kindness and charity to the former owners of the land, rather than as an act of justice, because there is no doubt, that when the Indians sold the reservation, and invested the proceeds, they intended to sell every deer, fish, bird, and mosquito on the whole tract. But it is an honor to the Legislature of that day that it was willing to make happy the last days of the New Jersey Indians by this act. That the Indians appreciated what had been done, may be seen from the following extract from a letter from Bartholomew Calvin : —

"Upon this parting occasion I feel it to be an incumbent duty to bear the feeble tribute of my praise to the high-toned justice of this State in dealing with the aboriginal inhabitants. Not a drop of our blood have you spilled in battle, not an acre of our land have you taken but by our consent. These facts speak for themselves, and need no comment. They place the character of New Jersey in bold relief, — a bright example to those States within whose territorial limits our brethren still remain. Nothing save benisons can fall upon her from the lips of a Lenni-Lenape."

But the love of their old home did not die out entirely in the hearts of all the Edge-Pillock Indians, who emigrated, first to New York, and then to Michigan. There was one Indian brave and his squaw, who, after living at Oneida for some time, began to long again for the old hunting ground in New Jersey; and, before the rest of their tribe went West, these two came back to Burlington County, and established themselves in a little house near Mount Holly. Here these two Indians lived for about twenty years; and when they died, they left a daughter, a tall powerful woman, known in the neighborhood as "Indian Ann," who for many years occupied the position of the last of the Lenni-Lenape in New Jersey.

She lived to be more than ninety years old; and her long straight black hair, her copper-colored skin, and bright eyes, gave the people of the neighborhood a good idea of what sort of people used to inhabit this country before their ancestors came over the sea. She had many true Indian character-istics, and loved to work in the open air better than to attend to domestic mat-ters in the house. Even when she was very old, she would go into the woods and cut down trees as if she had been a man. She did not die until December, 1894; and then the people who had known her so long gathered together at her funeral, and buried the last of the Indians of New Jersey.

Thus Scheyichbi, the land of the Indians, became truly and honestly New Jersey, the land of the Eng-lish settlers; and to this State belongs the honor of having been the first in the Union in which the set-tlers purchased and paid for the lands on which they settled, and in which the aboriginal owners were so fairly treated that every foot of the soil not purchased of them by individuals was bought and paid for by the government of the State.

FINS, RATTLES, AND WINGS.

WHEN the first settlers came to New Jersey, they found in that country plenty of wild animals, some of them desirable, and some quite otherwise. In the first class were great herds of red deer (especially in the central portion of the State), beavers, hares, and squirrels, and, among the dangerous kinds, bears, panthers, wolves, wild cats, and rattlesnakes. There were also many foxes, which were a great injury to the poultry yards of the settlers. Some of these creatures were so troublesome, that bounties were paid for the heads of panthers, foxes, and some other animals.

The white settlers found New Jersey a capital hunting ground. Nothing, however, that is told about hunting in the early days of New Jersey equals the accounts which are given of the fishing in the waters of that State. Soon after the settlement of Burlington, one of the townspeople wrote to his friends in England, describing the manner in which the people fished in that place.

The Delaware abounded in fish, and in the spring it swarmed with herring. When the early Burlingtonians wanted to catch herring, they did not trouble themselves about nets, or hooks and lines, but they built in the shallow water near the shore a pen, or, as they called it, a "pinfold," made by driving stakes into the sand so as to inclose a circular space about six feet in diameter. On the side toward the open water an aperture was left; and a big bush was made ready to close this up when the proper time came. Then the fishermen waded into the water, carrying with them great birch bushes. Sweeping the water with these, they slowly advanced toward the pinfold, driving swarms of herring before them, and so surrounding the frightened fish, that they had no way of escape, except by rushing through the entrance of the pinfold. Into the inclosure the shining creatures shot, — pushing, crowding, and dashing over each other, — until the pen was packed with fish, almost as closely jammed together as sardines in a tin box. Then the bush was driven down into the opening; and all that it was necessary to do, was to dip into the pinfold and take out great handfuls of fish. In this way bushels of herring could be procured at one time.

It is not to be supposed that in those days game fishing flourished to any extent; that is, sportsmen did not go out with rods and flies to catch little fish one at a time, when it was so easy to scoop them up by dozens.

Shad, too, were very abundant in those days, but not so highly valued as now. In fact, it is stated that when the settlers became more numerous, and the herring fewer, these fish were held in higher repute than shad; so that, when a man bought one hundred herring, he was expected to take ninety-five herring and five shad, or something in that proportion, shad being then rather a drug in the market.

In those early days there were denizens of the waters on the shores of New Jersey very much more valuable than herring, shad, or any other of these finny creatures, no matter in what dense throngs they might present themselves. These were whales, of which there were numbers in Delaware Bay, and even some distance up the river. When the Dutch De Vries first came into these waters, he came after whales; and even at the present day one of these great water monsters occasionally investigates the western coast of New Jersey, generally paying dear for his curiosity.

There were a great many snakes, many of them rattlesnakes, especially in the hilly country. The early settlers had a curious way of making themselves safe from these creatures. When they were going to make a journey through the woods or along wild country, where they expected to find snakes, they would take with them several hogs, and drive these grunting creatures in front of them. Hogs are very fond of eating snakes, and as they went along they would devour all they met with. It did not matter to the hogs whether the snakes were poisonous or harmless, they ate them all the same; for even the most venomous rattlesnake has but little chance against a porker in good condition, who, with his coat of bristles and the thick lining of fat under his skin, is so well protected against the fangs of the snake, that he pays no more attention to them than we to the seeds of a strawberry when we are eating one.

Rattlesnakes were in fact the most dangerous wild animals with which the early settlers had to contend; for they were very numerous, and their bite, if not treated properly at once, was generally fatal. The Indians, who well knew the habits of the snake, were not nearly as much afraid of it as were the whites.

In order to protect one's self against these creatures, unless there are too many of them, it is only necessary to make noise enough to let the snake know that some one is approaching, and it gets out of the way as fast as possible; or, if it has not time to do this, it coils itself up and springs its rattle, thus giving notice that it is on hand, and ready to strike.

It has often been said that the snake's rattle is for warning to birds and other animals; but this is now known to be a mistake, for when a snake rattles, it strikes its victim almost at the same time, if it has a chance.

It is now believed that the rattle is used to attract the attention of birds and other small creatures; and when they turn, and look into the eyes of the terrible serpent, they are so overcome with terror that they cannot fly away, and soon become its prey. This is commonly called snake charming; and a great many instances of it are related by people who are in the habit of telling the truth, and who have seen a snake charm a bird which could have flown away just as well as not, had it not been for the terrible attraction of those great eyes, which drew it nearer and nearer, until at last it found itself in the jaws of a snake.

The Indians did not give this significance to the rattle: they believed, as many people now do, that it was merely used as a warning. So, when an Indian met with a snake which rattled before he came up to it, he took it to be a snake of honest, straightforward principles, who wished to deceive nobody, and therefore gave fair notice of its presence. Such a serpent was never molested. But if a snake rattled

after an Indian had passed, the red man went back
and killed the creature, on the ground that it was
a sneak and a coward, which had neglected to give
warning to the passer-by.

A farmer living in Cumberland County tells a story
about having discovered an island in a swamp, which
so abounded in snakes, that he and some of his neighbors conceived the idea that this was the place where
they made their headquarters, and from which, in
summer time, they wandered to forage upon the country. The farmers waited until winter before they made
an attack upon this stronghold; and then they came
and dug up the ground, knowing that these reptiles
always pass the cold season in a torpid state underground.

It was not long before they came to what might be
called in these days a cold-storage vault. This was
a flat-bottomed cavity, filled to the depth of about three
inches with clear spring water; and in this water were
packed away a great number of snakes,
evenly laid side by side, so as to take up
as little room as possible. The majority of these creatures were rattlesnakes; but there were
black snakes among them, and one
large spotted snake. Besides these,
there were, as the narrator expressed it, at least a peck of
spring frogs; these having
probably crawled in to
fill up all corners and
vacant places. All these

reptiles were of course dormant and insensible, and were easily destroyed.

There is another story which gives even a better idea of the abundance of rattlesnakes in the new colony. In a quarry, from which the workmen were engaged in getting out stone for the foundations of Princeton College, a wide crack in the rocks was discovered, which led downward to a large cavity; and in this cave were found about twenty bushels of rattlesnake bones. There was no reason to believe that this was a snake cemetery, to which these creatures retired when they supposed they were approaching the end of their days; but it was, without doubt, a great rattlesnake trap. The winding narrow passage leading to it must have been very attractive to a snake seeking for retired quarters in which to take his long winter nap. Although the cave at the bottom of the great crack was easy enough to get into, it was so arranged that it was difficult, if not impossible, for a snake to get out of it, especially in the spring, when these creatures are very thin and weak, having been nourished all winter by their own fat. Thus year after year the rattlesnakes must have gone down into that cavity, without knowing that they could never get out again.

The great rivals, in point of numbers, to the herring and other fish in the rivers of New Jersey (and the snakes in their winter quarters underground), were the wild pigeons in the air. Several times in the year the settlers would be visited by vast flocks of these birds, which came in such numbers as to shut out the light of the sun, as if they had been clouds in the sky. They would remain in one place for a few days, and then pass on. As it was unnecessary to use hooks and lines to catch a few fish out of the multitudes which swarmed in the streams, so it was hardly worth while to waste powder and shot on the vast flocks of pigeons which visited New Jersey in those days. When they came to roost in the forests, they could be knocked down with poles and stones; and thousands and thousands of them were thus obtained by the men and boys, and very good eating they were.

There was a summer in which the settlers were very much astonished by the advent of a vast army of invaders to which they were not at all accustomed. These were locusts, probably of the kind we now call seventeen-year locusts; and the people were amazed to see these creatures come up out of the ground, clad in their horny coats of mail, which they afterwards cast off, when they appeared as winged creatures.

They could not understand how insects encumbered by such hard, unwieldy shells, could penetrate to such distance below the surface of the earth; for they did not know that each one of these locusts came from a little worm which had dropped into the ground many years before, and which had worked its way down to a great depth, and then, about a sixth of a century afterward, had reappeared on the surface as a hard-shell locust, ready to split its back, get out of its shell, spend a few days flying about in the summer air, lay its eggs in the twigs of trees, and then, having fulfilled all its duties on this earth, to die.

Although the farmers probably supposed that their crops would be eaten up by this vast horde of locusts, no great injury was done to them; for, as we now know, the seventeen-year locusts do not appear upon earth to destroy crops and vegetation, being far different from the grasshopper-like locusts which in our Western countries sometimes devastate large sections of farming lands. The twigs of the trees, which had been punctured in order that the eggs might be deposited, recovered their life, and put forth their leaves again when they had ceased to act as insect incubators.

THE STORY OF A GIRL AND A HOGS-HEAD.

SETTLERS came to New Jersey in various ways. Their voyages were generally very long, and it often happened that they did not settle at the place for which they had started, for there were many circumstances which might induce them to change their mind after they reached this country.

But there was one settler, and a very valuable one too, who came to New Jersey in an entirely original and novel fashion. She was a girl only sixteen years old, and a Swede. There is no reason to suppose that she wanted to come to America; but circumstances made it necessary that she should get out of Sweden, and this country was a very good place to come to. It is said that this girl, whose surname we do not know, but who was called Elizabeth, was a connection of the Swedish royal family; and, as there was great trouble at the time between different factions in the land, it happened that it was dangerous for Elizabeth to remain in Sweden, and it was very difficult to get her away. It is quite certain that she was a person of importance, because it was considered absolutely necessary to keep the authorities from knowing that she was about to sail for foreign lands.

There are people at the present day who, when they first go on board an ocean steamer, are very much surprised and disgusted at the small size of the stateroom they will have to occupy during the voyage; but if they could have seen the accommodations with which Elizabeth was obliged to content herself, they would not look with such contempt upon a room in which three persons can sleep, leaving space to move about.

The people who had Elizabeth's passage in charge conceived the idea that the safest way to get her on board the vessel, which was waiting at the dock, would be to ship her as freight. So she was put into a large hogshead, and securely fastened up, and then carried on board. She must have been a girl of a good deal of pluck, for the vessel was not to sail for several days, and she must remain in the hogshead all that time, as the officials of the port might come on board at any moment and discover her, if she should get out of her hiding place. I have no doubt that she was supplied with three or four meals a day through the bunghole.

Not only was Elizabeth's precious self thus duly consigned to America as if she had been ordinary merchandise, but a great many of her valuable possessions, jewels, clothes, etc., were also shipped to accompany her. In the course of time, and it must have been a dreary time to this poor girl, the ship moved out of the dock, and started on its voyage across the North Sea, and then over the Atlantic to the new country. Not until the vessel was well out

of sight of land, and free from danger of being overhauled by a vessel of the Swedish navy, did Elizabeth come out of her barrel and breathe the fresh
sea air.

At that time, early in the seventeenth century, a
good many vessels crossed the Atlantic, and most of
them must have made safe and successful
voyages; but it so happened that the
ship in which Elizabeth sailed was not
a fortunate craft. When she reached
the far-stretching Jersey coast, dangerous even now to mariners who know it
well, this vessel was overtaken by storm,
and soon became a hopeless wreck.

It might have been a very good
thing if Elizabeth had concluded
to end her voyage as she began it.
If she had put her valuables into
her hogshead, and then had jumped
in herself and had asked some of
the sailors to fasten her up, there
is no doubt that she would have
floated ashore, if she had known
how to keep the open bunghole
uppermost, — which no doubt she
did, — and would have saved all her possessions. If
one must float through stormy waves and great break-
ers, there is no safer way to do it than in a hogshead,
as has been proved by the man who in that way navi-
gated the fierce rapids at Niagara. But Elizabeth did
not go back to her hogshead. She took her chances

with the rest of the people on board, and with them was cast on the shore of New Jersey.

This shore was absolutely wild and bare, and what became of the others who reached it, we do not know; but Elizabeth eventually wandered off by herself, alone and lost in a strange land. If the people who had been so much concerned about her connection with the Swedish throne had been able to see her then, they would have been perfectly satisfied that she would give them no further trouble. How she lived during her days of wandering and solitude is not told; but when we remember that New Jersey is noted for its berries and for its clams, and that it was probably summer time when she was cast ashore (for mariners would generally calculate to arrive at the settlement in good weather), we may give a very good guess at Elizabeth's diet.

It was not very long before she found that there was another wanderer in this desolate and lonely place. She met with a white hunter named Garrison; and very much surprised must he have been when his eyes first fell upon her, — almost as much surprised, perhaps, as if he had come upon a stranded hogshead, with a human voice calling through the bunghole to be let out.

When a possible heiress of a royal crown meets with a solitary hunter, probably poor and of no family to speak of, her reception of him depends very much upon surrounding circumstances. In this case, those circumstances induced Elizabeth to look upon Garrison with more favor than she had ever looked upon a king or noble, for there is no doubt that she would have perished on that wild and uninhabited coast if she had not met with him.

Of course, the hunter gladly undertook to guide this Swedish girl to a settlement; and the two started off on their long tramp. It is not at all surprising that they soon began to like each other, that it was not long before they fell in love, and that in course of

time they were duly married. If she had ever thought of a marriage with a high-born Swede, Elizabeth gave up all such notions when she entered her hogshead, and left all her proud hopes behind her.

This young couple — one of royal Swedish blood, the other a hardy hunter of the New World — settled near Bridgeton, and there they flourished and prospered. Elizabeth lived to be ninety-five years old. She had ten children, and in 1860 it was computed that her descendants numbered at least a thousand. That any of these considered themselves better than their neighbors, because it was possible that they might have a drop or two of royal blood in their veins, is not likely; for but few American families would care to base their claims of social superiority upon such a very diluted foundation as this. But they would have good reason to trace with pride their descent from the plucky girl who started for America in a hogshead, and who was able to land alone and unassisted on the Jersey coast in a storm, and to take care of herself after she got ashore.

THE STORY OF PENELOPE STOUT

IN the early days of New Jersey, the Dutch settlers suffered very much from Indian hostilities. It was at the time that New Amsterdam, afterwards New York, was in the possession of the Dutch, that a ship came from Holland, bringing passengers who intended to settle in the new country. The ship was unfortunately wrecked in the neighborhood of Sandy Hook; but all the passengers managed to save themselves, and reached the shore.

Among these was a young couple whose names we do not know, except that the wife's maiden name was Penelope Van Princis. Her husband had been very sick during the voyage; and getting ashore through the surf from the wreck could not have been of any benefit to him, for, after he had reached dry land, he felt even worse than he had upon shipboard, and needed all the attention his wife could give him.

Although the passengers and crew of this vessel had reached the shore, they did not by any means consider themselves in safety; for they were very much afraid of the Indians, and desired above everything to make what haste they could toward New Amsterdam. They therefore started away as soon as possible. But Penelope's husband was too sick to go any farther at that time, and his wife was too good a woman to leave her husband in that lonely spot; and so these two were left behind, while the rest of the company started for New Amsterdam, promising, however, that they would send help to the unfortunate couple.

The fears of these immigrants in regard to the Indians were not without foundation; for the main party had not long departed, when a band of red men, probably having heard in some way of the wreck of the ship, appeared upon the scene, and discovered poor Penelope and her sick husband. It is unfortunately the disposition of most savages to show little pity for weakness and suffering, and the fact that the poor young man could not do them any possible harm had no effect upon them, and they set upon him and killed him; very much as a boy would kill a little harmless snake, for no reason whatever, except that he was able to do it.

Then they determined to kill Penelope also, and, attacking her with their tomahawks, they so cut and wounded her that she fell down bleeding and insensible. Having built a fire, these brave warriors cooked themselves a comfortable meal, and then departed. But Penelope was not killed, and, coming to her senses, her instincts told her that the first thing to do was to hide herself from these bloodthirsty red men: so, slowly and painfully, she crawled away to the edge of a wood, and found there a great hollow tree, into which she crept.

This made but narrow and doleful quarters for a wounded woman, but it was preferable at that time to the blue sky and fresh air. She did not leave the tree until nightfall, and then she made her way to the place where the fire was still glimmering; and by great care, and with what must have been painful labor, she kept this fire from going out, and so managed to get a little warmth.

In this way, living in the tree the greater part of the time, and depending for food chiefly upon the fungous excrescences and gum which grew on the outside of it, — for she was not able to go in search of berries and other food, — poor Penelope lived for a few days, with her dead husband on the beach, and her almost dead self in that cavern-like tree. The hours must have passed mournfully indeed to this young woman who had set out for the New World with such bright hopes.

That she survived her terrible hardships was due entirely to the existence of the danger she most feared; that is, the reappearance of the Indians. On the second morning, nearly famished and very weak, Penelope was making her way slowly over the ground, endeavoring to find something she could eat, or a little dew in the hollow of a leaf, that she might drink, when suddenly there came out of the woods two tall Indians, who, naturally enough, were much surprised to find a wounded white woman there alone upon the seashore.

Penelope gave herself up as lost. There was nothing now for her to do but to submit to her fate. It

was a pity, she thought, that she had not been slain
with her husband.

But the Indians did not immediately rush at her
with their tomahawks: they stood and talked together, evidently about her, with their fierce eyes
continually fixed upon her.
Then their conversation became more animated, and
it was soon plain that
they were disputing. Of
course, she did not then
know the cause of their
difference of opinion; but
she found out afterwards that one
of them was in favor of killing her
upon the spot, and the other, an older
man than his companion, was more
mercifully inclined, and wished to carry
her off as a prisoner to their camp.
At last the older man got the
better of the other one; and he,
being determined that the poor
wounded woman should be taken
care of, took her up and put her
on his shoulder, and marched away
with her. That an Indian should be able to perform
a feat like this is not at all surprising; for when one
of them shoots a deer in the forest, though many of
those animals are heavier than Penelope was, he will
put it on his back and carry it through the forests,
perhaps for miles, until he reaches his camp. And

so Penelope, as if she had been a deer wounded by some other hunters, which these men had found, was carried to the Indian camp.

There she was taken care of. Food and drink were given her. Her wounds were dressed and treated after the Indian fashion. In due course of time she recovered her health and strength, and there — living in a wigwam, among the women and children of the village, pounding corn, cooking food, carrying burdens as did the Indian women — she remained for some time, not daring even to try to escape; for in that wild country there was no place of safety to which it was possible for her to flee.

Although there was a good deal of bad feeling between the Indians and the whites at that time, they still traded and communicated with each other; and when, in the course of time, it became known in New Amsterdam that there was a white woman held as a prisoner in this Indian camp, there was every reason to suppose that this woman was the young wife who had been left on the seacoast by the survivors of the wreck. Consequently some of the men who had been her fellow-passengers came over to the Indian camp, which was not far from where Middletown now stands. Here, as they had expected, they found Penelope, and demanded that the Indians should give her up.

After some discussion, it was agreed that the matter should be left with Penelope herself; and the old Indian who had saved her life went to her, — for of course, being an inferior, she was not present at the conference,

— and put the question before her. Here she was, with a comfortable wigwam, plenty to eat and drink, good Indian clothes to wear, as well treated as any Indian woman, and, so far as he could see, with everything to make her comfortable and happy; and here she might stay if she chose. On the other hand, if she wished to go to New Amsterdam, she would find there no one with whom she was acquainted, except the people who had rowed away and left her on that desolate coast, and who might have come in search of her a long time before if they really had cared anything about her. If she wanted to live here among friends who had been kind to her, and be taken care of, she could do so; if she wanted to go away and live among people who had deserted her, and who appeared to have forgotten her, she could do that.

Very much to the surprise of this good Indian, Penelope declared that she should prefer to go and live among people of her own race and country; and so, much to the regret of her Indian friends, she departed for New Amsterdam with the men who had come for her.

A year or two after Penelope had gone back to New Amsterdam, being then about twenty-two, she married an Englishman named Richard Stout, who afterwards became an important personage. He, with other settlers, went over to New Jersey and founded a little village, which was called Middletown, not far from the Indian camp where Penelope had once been a prisoner. The Indians still remained in this camp, but now they appeared to be quite friendly to the whites; and the new settlers did not consider that there was anything dangerous in having these red neighbors. The good Indian who had been Penelope's protector, now quite an old man, was very friendly and sociable, and often used to visit Mrs. Stout. This friendship for the woman whom he had saved from death seemed to have been strong and sincere.

One day this old Indian came to the house of Mrs. Stout, and, seating himself in the room where she was, remained for a long time pensive and silent. This rather unusual conduct made Penelope fear that something had happened to him; and she questioned him, asking him why he was so silent, and why he sighed so often. Then the old man spoke out and told her that he had come on a very important errand, in which he had risked his own life at the hands of his tribe; but, having saved her life once, he had determined to do it again, no matter what might happen to himself.

Then he told her that the good will of the Indians toward their white neighbors had come to an end, and that it had been determined in council that an attack should be made that night upon this little village, when every person in it — men, women, and children — should be put to death, the houses burned, and the cattle driven away. His brethren no longer wanted white people living near them.

Of course, this news was a great shock to Penelope. She had now two little children, and she could not get far away with them and hide, as she herself had once hidden from Indian foes. But the old man told her that she need not be afraid : he could not save all the people in the village, but he was her friend, and he had arranged to save her and her family. At a certain place, which he described so she could not fail to find it, he had concealed a canoe ; and in that she and her husband, with the children, could go over to New Amsterdam, and there would be plenty of time for them to get away before the Indians would attack the place. Having said this, and having urged her to lose no time in getting away, the old Indian left.

As soon as he had gone, Penelope sent for her husband, who was working in the fields, and told him what she had heard, urging him to make preparations instantly to escape with her. But Mr. Stout was not easily frightened by news such as this. He pooh-poohed the whole story, and told his wife that the natives over there in their camp were as well disposed and friendly as if they had been a company of white settlers, and that, as these red men and the whites had lived together so long, trading with each other, and visiting each other with perfect freedom, there was no reason whatever to suppose that the Indians would suddenly determine to rise up and massacre a whole settlement of peaceable neighbors, who had never done them any harm, and who were a great benefit to them in the way of trading. It would be all nonsense, he said, to leave their homes, and run away from Indians so extremely friendly and good-natured as those in the neighboring camp.

But Penelope had entirely different ideas upon the subject. She thoroughly believed in the old Indian, and was sure that he would not have come and told her that story unless it had been true. If her husband chose to stay and risk his life, she could not help it; but she would not subject herself and her children to the terrible danger which threatened them. She had begged her husband to go with her; but as he had refused, and had returned to his work, she and her children would escape alone.

Consequently she set out with the little ones, and with all haste possible she reached the place where the canoe was moored among some tall reeds, and, getting in with the children, she paddled away to New Amsterdam, hoping she might reach there in time to send assistance to Middletown before the Indians should attack it.

When Farmer Stout found that his wife had really gone off, and had taken the children with her, he began to consider the matter seriously, and concluded that perhaps there might be something in the news which the old Indian had brought. He consequently called together a number of the men of the village, and they held a consultation, in which it was determined that it would be a wise thing to prepare themselves against the threatened attack; and, arming themselves with all the guns and pistols they could get, they met together in one of the houses, which was well adapted for that purpose, and prepared to watch all night.

They did not watch in vain, for about midnight they heard from the woods that dreadful war whoop which the white settlers now well understood. They knew it meant the same thing as the roar of the lion, who, after silently creeping towards his intended victim, suddenly makes the rocks echo with the sound of his terrible voice, and then gives his fatal spring.

But although these men might have been stricken with terror, had they heard such a war cry at a time when they were not expecting it, and from Indians to whom they were strangers, they were not so terrified at the coming of these red men with whom, perhaps only the day before, they had been trading buttons for venison and beans. They could not believe that these apparently mild and easy-going fellows could really be the terrible savages they tried to make themselves appear.

So Richard Stout and his companions went boldly out, guns in hand, to meet the oncoming savages, and, calling a parley, they declared that they had no intention of resting quietly, and allowing themselves and families to be slaughtered and their houses burned. If the Indians, who had so long been their good neighbors, were now determined to become bloody enemies, they would find that they would have to do a good deal of hard fighting before they could destroy the village of Middletown; and, if they persisted in carrying on the bloody job they had undertaken, a good many of them would be killed before that job was finished.

Now, it had been very seldom that Indians who had started out to massacre whites had met with people who acted like this; and these red men in war paint thought it wise to consider what had been said to them. A few of them may have had guns, but the majority were armed only with bows and tomahawks; and these white men had guns and pistols, with plenty of powder and ball. It would clearly be unsafe to fight them.

So, after discussing the matter among themselves and afterwards talking it over with the whites, the Indians made up their minds, that, instead of endeavoring to destroy the inhabitants of Middletown, they would shake hands with them and make a treaty of peace. They then retired; and on the following day a general conference was held, in which the whites agreed to buy the lands on which they had built their town, and an alliance was made for mutual protection and assistance. This compact was faithfully observed as long as there were any Indians in the neighborhood, and Middletown grew and flourished.

Among the citizens of the place there were none who grew and flourished in a greater degree than the Stout family. Although Penelope bore upon her body the scars of her wounds until the day of her death, it is stated, upon good authority, that she lived to be one hundred and ten years old; so that it is plain that her constitution was not injured by the sufferings and hardships of the beginning of her life in New Jersey.

Not only did the Stouts flourish in Middletown, but some of them went a little southward, and helped to found the town of Hopewell; and here they increased to such a degree that one of the early historians relates that the Baptist Church there was founded by the Stouts, and that for forty-one years the religious meetings were held in the houses of different members of the Stout family, while, at the time he wrote, half of the congregation of the church were still Stouts, and that, all in all, there had been at least two hundred members of that name. So the Baptist Church in Hopewell, as well as all the churches in Middletown, owed a great deal to the good Indian who carried poor Penelope to his village, and cured her of her wounds.

THE SCHOOLMASTER AND THE DOCTOR.

O F course, it was not long after New Jersey began to be settled and cultivated, before there were a great many boys and girls who also needed to be cultivated. And if we are to judge their numbers by the families of Elizabeth, who started for the New World in a hogshead, and of Penelope, who began her life here in a hollow tree, there must have been an early opportunity for the establishment of flourishing schools; that is, so far as numbers of scholars make schools flourishing.

But in fact it does not appear that very early attention was given in this State to the education of the young. The first school of which we hear was established in 1664; but it is probable that the first settlers of New Jersey were not allowed to grow up to be over forty years old before they had any chance of going to school, and it is likely that there were small schools in various places of which no historical mention is made.

It is admitted, however, by the historians of these early days of New Jersey, that education was not attended to as it should have been; and we read that in 1693 an act was passed to "establish schoolmasters within the Province, 'for the cultivation of learning and good manners for the good and benefit of mankind, which hath hitherto been much neglected in the Province.'"

These early schools were not of a very high order; the books used by younger scholars being what were called hornbooks, which were made by pasting upon a board a piece of paper containing the alphabet and some lessons in spelling, and covering the whole with a very thin sheet of horn, which was fastened on the board as glass is fastened over a framed picture. Thus the children could see the letters and words under the horn. but were not able to deface or tear the paper. It was difficult to get books in those days, and a hornbook would last a long time.

We can get a pretty good idea of the character of the schools from an account given of the establishment of the first school in Newark, where the town authorities made a contract "with Mr. John Catlin to instruct their children and servants in as much English, reading, writing, and arithmetic, as he could teach."

But the people of New Jersey prospered well, and the Colony soon became noted as one in which there was comfort and good living ; and therefore it is natural that when the people really could afford to apply their time, thought, and money to objects higher than the tillage of farms and the building of houses, they went to work earnestly to give their young people proper opportunities for education, and we find that they were inclined to do this as earnestly and thoroughly as they had been in the habit of doing other things.

In consequence of this disposition, what is now Princeton College was founded in 1746. This institution was first called the "College of New Jersey," and was established at Elizabethtown. It was in its early days a very small seat of learning; for, when the Rev. Mr. Dickinson was appointed to be its president, the faculty consisted entirely of himself, and his only assistant was an usher. There were then about twenty students in the college.

In about a year the president died; and the college was then removed to Newark, where the Rev. Aaron Burr, the father of the celebrated Aaron Burr, became its president, and it is probable that the faculty was enlarged. Ten years afterwards the college was established at Princeton.

The manners and customs of the college must have been very primitive, and we will give a few of the rules which were made for the students: "Every scholar shall keep his hat off to the president about ten rods, and about five to the tutors. When walking with a superior, they shall give him the highest place, and when first going into his company, they shall show their respects to him by first pulling off their hats; shall give place to him at any door or entrance; or meeting him going up and down stairs shall stop, giving him the bannister side;" and, in speaking to a superior, "shall always give a direct and pertinent answer, concluding with Sir." Thus it is seen that attention to good manners was one of the most important branches of study taught at the young college.

But in certain districts of New Jersey, people seemed to be very slow in perceiving the advantages of schools in their midst. Schools had sprung up here and there in towns and villages, many of them boarding schools; and to these the richer farmers would send their children. But it took people in some rural places a good while to find out that it would be a good thing to have a school in their midst.

A story is told of the establishment of a school of this kind in Deckertown as late as 1833. The people of this village had never thought it worth while to have a school of their own; and even after a gentleman of learning and ability, who was well known in the place, offered to take charge of such a school, they did not look with any favor upon the enterprise. The only place for a schoolhouse, which he was able to obtain, was a very small building, consisting of one room, and situated on the outskirts of the town. Here he started a school with one scholar; and even this little fellow was not a Jersey boy, but came from New York.

For a considerable time this single scholar constituted the school, and he and the schoolmaster walked back and forth from the village to the little cabin every day; while the only interest that the townspeople seemed to take in them was shown by their laughing at the schoolmaster, and comparing him to a hen with one chicken. It must not be supposed that it was because the citizens did not believe in education; but, as they had been in the habit of sending their children away to school, they thought that

that was the proper thing to do, and, as there never had been a school in the town, they saw no reason why there should be one then. But the school increased, and in less than a year it numbered twenty scholars.

There is a rather peculiar story told of this school in its early days. It had been established about two months, when the schoolmaster happened to be walking in the direction of the school quite late in the evening, and to his amazement he saw that the little room was brilliantly lighted. Now, as he and his scholar had left it in the afternoon, and he had locked the door, he could not understand the state of affairs. Hurrying to the house, he looked in at the window, and saw that the room was nearly filled with well-dressed men, who were standing and sitting around a table on which were spread cards and money. He saw that they were a company of gamblers; but how they came there, and why they came, he could not imagine. Of course, he could not drive them out; but, after watching them for a little while, he boldly opened the door and went in among them.

They were so occupied with their game, however, that they paid little attention to him; and, after standing with them for a time, he remarked to one of them that he hoped that when they had finished their game, and were ready to go away, they would leave everything behind them in as good order as they had found it, and then he himself departed and went home. But the next morning, when he and his scholar came to the schoolhouse, he found everything as they had left it on the afternoon before; and this schoolmaster might have been excused if he had imagined that he had dreamed that he saw the curious sight of a company of gamblers in his schoolhouse.

But he found out afterwards that it was no dream. There was a set of men gathered together from the neighboring country, who regularly spent certain evenings in gambling for high stakes. They had discovered that there was no better place for their meetings than the little schoolhouse, which was tenanted by two persons in the daytime and by nobody at night; and, as it was so far away from the other houses, it was a very convenient place for their secret meetings, and they had been in the habit of assembling there almost from the very time that it was cleaned out and arranged for a schoolhouse.

When the schoolmaster found that he had devoted his energies to the establishment of a very flourishing gambling saloon, when he supposed that he had founded nothing but a weak little school, he took measures to prevent any further visits from the gentlemen with the cards and the money. After that, the exercises in addition, subtraction, and multiplication, were figured out with a pencil or chalk instead of being done by means of spades or diamonds.

In those early days the doctor was almost as slow in coming to the front as was the schoolmaster.

In fact, it is said that the first doctors in New Jersey were women, and that the people placed such faith in their abilities, that unless a case were very serious indeed, so that a physician had to be sent for from the city, they were perfectly satisfied with the services of the women doctors. It is also stated, that in those days the people of New Jersey were very healthy. These two statements can be put together in different ways: some may say, that, where people were so seldom sick, doctors of great ability were not needed; while, on the other hand, those who have a higher opinion of womankind might well believe, that, because women made such good doctors, the people were seldom sick.

It must be remembered, however, that the mothers, wives, sisters, and daughters of the people of this State, were formerly looked upon as of more importance than they are now; and among the rights which they possessed in those early days, but of which they have since been deprived, was the right of voting. An early writer, speaking of this privilege, says, "The New Jersey women, however, showed themselves worthy of the respect of their countrymen by generally declining to avail themselves of this preposterous proof of it." It is very pleasant for us to remember that New Jersey was among the first of our States in which free and equal rights were given to all citizens, male or female, if they chose to avail themselves of them.

But when the population of New Jersey so increased that it became plain that the women could not be physicians, and attend at the same time to their domestic duties, the care of their children, and the demands of society, the citizens of New Jersey gave as earnest and thorough attention to their needs in the way of medicine and surgery as they had given to their needs in the way of college education; and the first State Medical Society in this country was founded in New Jersey in the year 1766.

It is said that some of the early doctors of New Jersey possessed great ability, and, although there could not have been many of them at first, they arranged for a suitable increase in their society, and nearly every one of them had one or more students.

A medical student in those days did not occupy the same position that he holds now. In fact, he was nothing more nor less than an apprentice to his master. He was bound to the doctor by a regular indenture. He lived in his family, and, when he was not engaged in his studies, he was expected to make himself useful in various domestic ways, often learning the use of the saw in the wood yard.

A very natural consequence of this domestic fashion of pursuing their studies was, that, when the young doctor started out to establish a practice for himself, he not only had a certificate or diploma from his master, but was also provided with a wife, for marriages of medical students with the daughters of their preceptors were very common.

What further outfit was furnished a student setting out in practice for himself, may be imagined from the conclusion of an old indenture of apprenticeship, which states, that when Jacobus Hubbard shall have fulfilled his apprenticeship of four years and eight months, — during which he has well and faithfully served his master, his secrets kept, his lawful commands gladly everywhere obeyed, — he shall be provided, when he goes forth as doctor, with a "new set of surgeon's pocket instruments, Solomon's Dispensatory, Quence's Dispensatory, and Fuller on Fevers."

It is probable that such a very healthy country as New Jersey did not always give a doctor of a neighborhood sufficient work to occupy his time, and therefore the early physicians used to combine other professions with that of medicine and surgery. Some were lawyers, others clergymen, and many were farmers and planters. The following story is told about the Rev. Jacob Green, "who lived in Hanover, and was pastor of the Presbyterian Church in that place. He had also many other callings, as may be inferred from a letter addressed to him by a wag, and which was said not to exaggerate the truth: —

"'To the Rev. Jacob Green, *Preacher*.
"   "   "   "   *Teacher*.
"   "   "   "   *Doctor*.
"   "   "   "   *Proctor*.
"   "   "   "   *Miller*.
"   "   "   "   *Distiller*.'"

The necessity for this variety of occupation is shown by a letter from a gentleman named Charles Gordon, living near Plainfield, to his brother, Dr. John Gordon, in England, in which he says, "If you design to come hither, you may come as a planter or merchant; but as a doctor of medicine I cannot advise you, for I hear of no diseases to cure but some agues and some cutted legs and fingers." Other physicians gave up their professions at the beginning of the Revolution, and became prominent in military matters.

Dr. John Cochran, one of the first New Jersey physicians, was a man of wide experience and reputation. He was surgeon in the British hospital during the French War, and afterward practiced medicine in New Brunswick. During the Revolution, he became an army surgeon. He was a friend of Washington, and, in fact, was quite intimate with the commander in chief of the American forces. It is said that when Washington was at West Point in 1779, and the doctor and his family were stationed at the same place, Washington wrote to Dr. Cochran almost the only facetious letter which is known to have come from the pen of that grave and dignified man.

This letter informs the doctor that he has invited Mrs. Cochran and Mrs. Livingston to dine with him the next day, and says that the table is large enough for the ladies, and then proceeds to tell "how it is covered." "Since our arrival at this happy spot, we have had a ham, sometimes a shoulder of bacon, to grace the head of the table; a piece of roast beef adorns the foot, and a dish of beans or greens, almost imperceptible, decorates the center. When the cook has a mind to cut a figure, which I presume will be the case to-morrow, we have two beefsteak pies, or dishes of crabs, in addition, one on each side of the center dish, dividing the space, and reducing the distance between dish and dish to about six feet, which without them would be twelve feet apart. Of late, he has had the surprising sagacity to discover that apples will make pies, and it is a question if in the violence of his efforts we do not get one of apples instead of having both of beefsteak. If the ladies can put up with such entertainment, and will submit to partake of it on plates once tin, now iron (not become so by scouring), I shall be happy to see them."

The fact that the early physicians of New Jersey were very skillful, and patients in that healthful country very scarce, seems to have had the effect of making some physicians of that day extremely sharp about business matters. A certain doctor of Rahway had been called upon to visit a rich man who was in great pain and distress. The doctor having administered some medicine, the patient very speedily recovered. Some time after this, the doctor determined to leave Rahway; and the rich man who had been attended by him with such gratifying results began to be afraid that he might be taken sick again in the same way. So he went to the doctor, and requested that before he left, he would give him the prescription which had seemed to suit his case so admirably.

Doctors seldom approve of their patients taking their treatment into their own hands; but, after a little consideration, he said he would furnish the prescription, but that it would cost ten dollars. This quite astonished the rich man, and at first he refused to pay such a high price; but, after considering that it might save him many visits from the new doctor who should come to Rahway, he agreed to pay the price demanded, and the prescription was written, and delivered to him. When he reached his home, he thought he would try to make out what this prescription was; but when he opened the paper, he found nothing but the word "catnip." It is not likely that he ever again tried to take advantage of the medical profession.

But it was not always Jersey doctors whose wit shone brightest in a financial transaction. There was a doctor in the town of Rocky Hill who was sent for to attend a poor old man who was suffering with a piece of bone sticking in his throat. The doctor went immediately to the old man's house, and it was not long before the bone was out. As the doctor was packing up his instruments, the old fellow, whose name was William, inquired how much he would have to pay; and the doctor replied that for an operation of that sort his charge was five dollars. This quite astonished William, who probably had not five cents in the house; but he wished to pay his debts, and not to be considered a pauper patient, and so he asked the doctor if he might come to his house and work out the bill. The doctor replied that that would be entirely satisfactory to him, and that William might come the next day and work in the garden.

The next day old William went to the doctor's house. All day he faithfully dug and hoed and raked. Toward the end of the afternoon the doctor came into the garden, and, after informing William that he might come again, he casually asked him how much he charged for a day's work. William stood up and promptly answered, that for a day's labor in the garden his charge was five dollars. Now was the doctor surprised.

"You don't mean," he exclaimed, "that you are going to ask five dollars for one day's labor!"

"That is exactly my price," said William. "If two minutes' yanking with a pair of pincers at a little bone is worth five dollars, then one day's hard labor in tilling the ground is worth just as much."

It often happens that doctors are men of wit and humor; and it is recorded that a New Jersey physician, named Dr. Hole, was the author of the first version of a tombstone epitaph which afterwards became widely known and used. The lines of Dr. Hole are cut upon a tombstone of a child, and run as follows: —

"A dropsy sore long time I bore:
  Forsitions were in vain
Till God above did hear my moan,
  And eased me of my pain."

That some of those early doctors were honest is proved by a doctor's bill which is now preserved in the New Jersey Historical Society. At the end of this bill, after all the different items of service and medicine had been charged upon it, there is this entry: "Contrary credit by Medsons brought back." It would be difficult now to find a doctor in New Jersey, or anywhere else, who would be willing to take back, and allow credit for, all partly filled bottles of medicine, and boxes of pills, the contents of which had been ordered, but not entirely used.

THE SLAVES OF NEW JERSEY.

WE have so long looked upon New Jersey as prominent among what were called the "free States" of the Union, that it now seems strange when we consider, that among the first of the institutions established upon its soil by the early settlers, was the system of slavery. This was the case not only in New Jersey, but in all the American Colonies. The settlers of New England, as well as those of the Southern Colonies, used negro slaves as laborers on their farms; and the trade in native Africans was a very important branch of industry.

The Duke of York, to whom his brother, Charles II.,

had made a grant of extensive American possessions, was at the head of the African Company, formed for the purpose of bringing slaves from Africa, and selling them. The Dutch were then the great rivals of the English in this trade; and the Duke of York was very glad to possess New Jersey and the rest of his grant, for then he could not only oust the Dutch from the territory, but could possess himself of this very desirable and profitable slave market.

But it was not only the English and Dutch who brought negro slaves to America, for it is stated that the earliest Swedish settlers brought slaves with them as laborers. So we may say that slavery and freedom were planted together in this country of ours; one to be pulled up afterward like a weed, the other to be left to grow and flourish.

When Berkeley and Carteret acquired authority over New Jersey, they did everything that they could to induce settlers to come to the new country; and, as they were anxious to have the lands opened up and cultivated as rapidly as possible, they encouraged immigrants to bring as many slaves as they could afford. They offered one hundred and fifty acres to every one who would settle, and another one hundred and fifty acres for every full-grown able-bodied male slave, and seventy-five acres each for those not grown up. Afterwards, when slaves became more numerous, the bounties given on their account were diminished, and in course of time they ceased altogether.

A great many slaves must have been brought direct from Africa to New Jersey, for at Perth Amboy there was established what was then called a barracks; and in this, negroes who had been brought in the slave ships were confined until they were sold and sent out into the country.

Not only were there negro slaves in the State, but there were also Indians who had been enslaved, and were regularly sold and bought. How these red men happened to be slaves, we do not certainly know; but we may be very sure that the whites did not make war upon Indian tribes, and capture prisoners, for the purpose of making slaves of them. It is far more likely, that, when one tribe of Indians made war upon another, the conquerors found it a very profitable thing

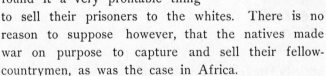

to sell their prisoners to the whites. There is no reason to suppose however, that the natives made war on purpose to capture and sell their fellow-countrymen, as was the case in Africa.

The early records, however, prove that there were Indian slaves. When the House of Representatives for the Province met at Burlington in 1704, an act was brought before that body for the regulating of Indian and negro slaves.

Negroes were then considered to be such legitimate articles of merchandise, that English sovereigns thought it very necessary to see to it that their loyal settlers were sufficiently supplied with slaves, and at prices not too high. When Queen Anne sent out Lord Cornbury as governor of the Province, she recommended the Royal African Company to the especial attention of the governor, that New Jersey might have a constant and sufficient supply of merchantable negroes at moderate rates in money or commodities. In consequence of the fostering care of the Proprietors and the English sovereigns, slaves rapidly increased in New Jersey.

The English themselves were not at all averse to the ownership of a good serviceable slave; and about the middle of the eighteenth century a young gentleman in England wrote to his father in New Jersey, begging that he might "be favored with a young negro boy to present to the brother of the then Duke of Grafton, to whom he was under obligations, as 'a present of that kind would be very acceptable.'"

Of course, the existence of slavery made the state of society in New Jersey and the other Colonies very different from what it is now; and this difference is strongly shown by the advertisements of runaway negroes, which we can find in some old newspapers. It seems very strange to see in a Boston paper of one hundred years ago a picture of a black man running away with a bag over his shoulder, and under the picture the statement of the reward which would be given for his capture; and in the New Jersey papers there were frequent advertisements of runaway slaves and of negroes for sale. One of these, published in Burlington two years after the Colony had declared itself free and independent, reads as follows: —

"TO BE SOLD — For no fault — but a saucy tongue for which he is now in Burlington jail — A negro man about 39 years of age. He is a compleat farmer, honest and sober. For further particulars enquire of the subscriber in Evesham, Burlington Co. Feb. 4, 1778."

When Washington was in Morristown in 1777, one of his aids wrote a letter to a friend in Elizabethtown, which states, —

The General will esteem it as a singular favor if you can apprehend a mulatto girl, servant and slave of Mrs. Washington, who eloped from this place yesterday, with what design cannot be conjectured, though as she may intend to the enemy and pass your way I trouble you with the description : her name is Charlotte but in all probability will change it, yet may be discovered by question. She is light complected, about thirteen years of age, pert, dressed in brown cloth wescoat and petticoat. Your falling upon some method of recovering her should she be near you will accommodate Mrs. Washington and lay her under great obligations to you being the only female servant she brought from home and intending to be off to-day had she not been missing. A gentle reward will be given to any soldier or other who shall take her up.

I am with respect your most obedient servant

After a time, negro slaves became so plentiful in New Jersey, that laws were passed restricting their importation, and a considerable tax was laid upon each African brought into the country.

But the negroes were not the only slaves in New Jersey during those early days. Here, as well as in many of the other Colonies, was a class of white people, generally from England, who were called "redemptioners." These were poor people, although often persons of fairly good station and education, who desired to emigrate to America, but who could not afford to pay their passage.

A regular system was then established, by which a poor person desiring to settle in New Jersey would be brought over free. When one of these emigrants took passage on a ship, he signed a contract which gave the captain of the vessel the right to sell him, as soon as he arrived in America, for enough money to pay his passage. This white man was thus bought, when he reached New Jersey, exactly as if he had been a negro slave; and he was subject to the same rules as those which governed other slaves. Of course, he was made the subject of great imposition; for the captain would naturally desire to get as large a sum of money as possible for each redemptioner, and therefore would be perfectly willing to sell him for a long term.

The people who owned redemptioners could sell them again if they chose; and it often happened that some of them passed into the possession of several families before they finally served out the term for which they had been sold. All sorts of people became redemptioners, — mechanics, laborers, and even professional men. Among the people who sold themselves into limited slavery there were schoolmasters, and it is stated that at one time the supply of redemptioner schoolmasters was so great that they became a drug in the market.

In the days before there were many regular schools in New Jersey, much of the education must have been carried on by what we now call private tutors; and a schoolmaster who could be bought as if he had been

a horse or a cow was often a very convenient piece of property. If a family should own a teacher who was able only to instruct small children, it would be very easy, when these children grew older and able to undertake more advanced studies, to sell this primary teacher to some family where there were young pupils, and buy one capable of teaching higher branches.

It is said that these redemptioners were often treated

much more harshly and cruelly than the negro slaves, and any one who assisted one of them to escape was severely punished. There was good reason for this difference in the treatment of the two classes of slaves; for a negro was the property of his master as long as he lived, and it was manifestly the interest of the owner to keep his slave in good condition. But the redemptioner could only be held for a certain time, and, if his master was not a good man, he would be apt to get out of him all the work that he could during the time of his service, and to give him no more food or clothing than was absolutely necessary.

After a time there were laws made to protect the redemptioners. One of these was, that any person sold after he was seventeen years old could not serve for more than four years; and another provided, that, when a redemptioner's time of service had expired, his master should give him "two good suits of clothing, suitable for a servant, one good ax, one good hoe,. and seven bushels of Indian corn."

But although the redemptioner sometimes fared very badly in the new country, it often happened that he came out very well in the end. Among the white people who came here as slaves there were often convicts and paupers; but even some of these succeeded in bettering their condition and establishing themselves as good citizens, and in founding families.

It often happened that some of the Germans who came to buy land and settle, chose rather to put away their money, and sell themselves as redemptioners to English families, so that they might learn the English language and manner of living. Then, when they had educated themselves in this practical manner, and their time of service was over, they could buy land, and establish themselves on terms of equality with their English neighbors.

But the trade in redemptioners gradually decreased; and by the middle of the eighteenth century there were not many of them left in New Jersey, although there were a few in the State until after the Revolution. Negro slavery, however, continued much longer. It grew and flourished until it became a part of the New Jersey social system; but it must not be supposed that all the people of the State continued to be satisfied with this condition of things.

At first everybody who could afford it owned slaves, and the Friends or Quakers bought negroes the same as other people did; but about the end of the seventeenth century some of these Quakers began to think that property in human beings was not a righteous thing, and the Quakers of New Jersey united with those of Pennsylvania in an agreement recommending to the members of the Society of Friends that they should no longer employ negro slaves, or, if they thought it best to continue to do this, that they should at least cease to import them.

A strong party among the Quakers of New Jersey opposed slavery for many years, and the system was denounced at some of their yearly meetings; and this went on until about the middle of the next century, when a law was made that no person owning slaves should continue in the Society of Friends.

As years passed on, people other than Quakers began to consider slavery an injustice and an evil; and this feeling gradually increased, until in the beginning of the nineteenth century it became very strong, and in 1820 an act was passed by the Legislature for the emancipation of the slaves. They were not set free all at once, and turned into the world to take care of themselves; but a system of gradual emancipation was adopted, by which the young people obtained their freedom when they came of age, while the masters were obliged to take care of the old negroes as long as they lived. By this plan, slavery was very gradually abolished in New Jersey, so that in 1840 there were still six hundred and seventy-four slaves in the State; and even in 1860 eighteen slaves remained, and these must have been very old.

A JERSEY TEA PARTY.

A T the time when the American colonists began to be restless under the rule of Great Britain, the people of New Jersey showed as strong a desire for independence as those of any other Colony, and they were by no means backward in submitting to any privations which might be necessary in order to assert their principles. As has been said before, the people were prosperous, and accustomed to good living, and it was not likely that there was any part of America in which a cup of well-flavored tea was better appreciated than in New Jersey.

But when the other colonists determined to resist unjust taxation, and resolved that they would not use tea, on which a heavy tax was laid without allowing the American people to have anything to say about it, the patriotic people of New Jersey resolved that they too would use no tea so long as this unjust tax was placed upon it. When the tea was destroyed in Boston Harbor, the Jersey patriots applauded the act, and would have been glad to show in the same way what they thought upon the subject.

But when tea was shipped from England, it was sent to the great ports of Boston, New York, Philadelphia, and Charleston; and what was used in New Jersey came from these places after the consignees had paid the tax. However, to show their sympathy with the efforts which were being made at the seaports to prevent the landing of tea, the New Jersey people, that is, those who belonged to the Whig party, — which was the patriotic party, and opposed to the Tories, who favored England, — formed an association, the members of which bound themselves to buy or use no tea until the tax should be removed.

There is a story told of Hugh Drum of Somerset County, who was so thoroughly in earnest on this subject, and who probably supposed that the weak little Colonies would always have to submit to the power of Great Britain, that he took an oath that never again during the rest of his life would he take a cup of tea; and although he lived a great many years afterward, during which the Americans imported their own tea without regard to what any other country thought about it, Mr. Drum never again drank tea.

But at last an opportunity came for patriotic Jerseymen to show that they were not behind the other colonists in resisting the attempt of Great Britain to force upon them this taxed tea.

Nearly a year after the tea had been thrown overboard in Boston Harbor, a vessel from England — loaded with tea, and bound to Philadelphia — put into Cohansey Creek, a small stream which runs into Delaware Bay, and anchored at the little town of Greenwich. This vessel, called the "Greyhound," was afraid to go

up to Philadelphia, because from that port tea ships
were sent back to England as soon as they arrived,
as was also the case in New York. So the captain
of the "Greyhound" thought it would be a good plan
to land his tea at Greenwich, from which place it
could be taken inland to its destination. Here the
cargo was unloaded, and stored in the cellar of a
house opposite the open market place.

This business of forcing tea upon the American
colonists had become a very serious matter to England; for the East India Company had now in their
warehouses at London seventeen million pounds of
tea, and, if there should be no sale for any of this
in the American market, the loss would be very severe.
Consequently every possible method was resorted to,
in order to have the tea landed on American soil; it
being believed, that, if the tea once got into the hands
of the dealers, the people would overcome their prejudices to its importation, and begin to use it again.

Therefore the captain of the "Greyhound" thought
he was doing a very sharp thing when he sailed up
Cohansey Creek and unloaded his tea. That cargo
was landed, and in those days an English captain of
a tea ship might well be proud of having performed
such a feat.

But it is not likely that the captain of the "Greyhound" had ever before sailed into a port of New
Jersey, large or small, or had anything to do with
Jerseymen; for if he had, he would not have been
so well satisfied with the result of the voyage.

The people of Greenwich could not prevent the

landing of the tea, for there was no organized force at the place, nor could they order the "Greyhound" to turn round and go back to England; but they would not allow their town to be made use of as a port of entry for this obnoxious merchandise, simply because it was a little town, and could not keep English ships out of its waters. A meeting of the patriotic citizens was held, and it was resolved that no tea should go out of Greenwich to comfort the bodies and contaminate the principles of people in any part of the Colonies; and they would show their British tyrants that it was just as unsafe to send tea into Cohansey Creek as it was to send it into the harbor of Boston.

Having come to this determination, they went immediately to work. A party of young men, about forty in number, was organized; and in order to disguise themselves, or strike terror into anybody who might be inclined to oppose their undertaking, they were all dressed as Indians. They assembled in the market place, and then, making a rush to the house in which the tea was stored, they broke open the doors, carried out the tea, split open the boxes in which it was contained, and made a great pile of it in an open space near by.

When tea is dry and in good condition, it will burn very well, and it was not many minutes before there was a magnificent bonfire near the market place in Greenwich; and in all that town there was not one man who dared to attempt to put it out. Thus the cargo of the "Greyhound" went up in smoke to the sky. It must have been a very hard thing for the good ladies of the town to sit in their houses and sniff the delightful odor, which recalled to their minds the cherished beverage, of which, perhaps, they might never again partake. But they were Jerseywomen, of stout hearts and firm principles, and there is no record that any one of them uttered a word of complaint.

But in every community there is at least one person in whose mind there is a little streak of the Ananias nature, and there was a man of that kind in Greenwich. His name was Stacks, and he was a great lover of tea; moreover, he had a soul disposed to economy and thrift. Consequently it was very hard for him to stand by and see all that tea wasted; and he thought it would be no harm — as he was not a merchant, and did not intend to exercise evil influences upon the people of America by inducing them to buy tea — if he appropriated to himself a little of this most desirable herb, which was to be burned and wasted before his very eyes.

Whenever he had a chance, he slipped a little tea into some part of his clothes where he thought it would not be noticed, and so gradually loaded himself with a considerable stock of the herb. In fact, he stowed away so many handfuls of it, that, when the fire was over, his companions noticed that he had considerably increased in size; and it was not long before his trick was discovered. We do not hear that he was compelled to empty out the tea, but we are told that ever after he went by the name of "Tea Stacks."

This tea bonfire created a great stir, and although the patriotic party approved it, there were a great many Tories in the country who condemned it as a piece of outrageous violence and wanton waste. This latter opinion was so freely expressed, that the English owners of the cargo were encouraged to take legal steps against the men who destroyed the tea. It was easy enough to do this; for the young fellows who had made the bonfire were very proud of what they had done, and, instead of denying their connection with the burning of the tea, were always very ready to boast of it.

When it was understood that the tea burners were to be prosecuted, all the Whigs of the surrounding country determined to stand by them; and they subscribed a large sum of money to engage lawyers to defend their case. The strength of the popular feeling was shown by the fact, that, when the case was brought to court, the grand jury positively refused to bring a bill against these young men, although the judge insisted that they should do so. The matter was thus postponed; and as it was not long before the Colonies

Tea Stacks.

broke out into open rebellion, and a period followed when Englishmen no longer brought suits in American courts, there was no further action in regard to the tea burning at Greenwich.

Therefore, unless Mr. Stacks contrived to keep some of the tea which he carried off in his clothes, the good people of the neighborhood, if they drank tea at all, made it of the dried leaves of raspberries, or those of some other bush, which have something of a tea taste, and were thus enabled to have a hot beverage with their evening meal, with but a little strain upon their imaginations, and none at all on their consciences.

In other neighborhoods, however, there were people who, although they were patriots and inclined to support the cause of American liberty, could not see how such a little thing as drinking a cup of tea, if they happened to have it, could interfere with their regard and respect for the great principle of justice and independence.

Of course, it was to be supposed that the Tories, who were opposed to this nonsense about independence, were glad to buy tea and to drink it whenever they got the chance; but it was expected that those who called themselves Whigs and patriots would stand by their party, and discountenance tea drinking. There is a story told of a man who lived in Bridgetown, who was a member of one of the Committees of Safety which were formed for the purpose of promoting the cause of American liberty. It was found out that this man and his family were in the habit ot drinking East India tea; and when his fellow-committeemen asked him in regard to this matter, he boldly admitted that they all liked tea, that they drank tea, and that they intended to drink tea.

This was a very serious matter, and the committee saw that it was necessary to take vigorous measures in regard to this peculiar case. At first they tried the force of argument; but all they could say to the man amounted to nothing. He had principles, and what he considered very good principles; but he liked tea, and, having it in the house, he saw no harm in drinking it. So the teapot was on his table every day.

Now, his fellow-committeemen held another meeting, and formally resolved that this unpatriotic patriot should be punished in a way which would make a powerful impression on him, and which would show the whole community how the Committee of Safety intended to stand firm in the position they had taken in resisting unjust legislation. It was resolved, that, so long as he and his family drank tea, the patriots of the neighborhood would have nothing to do with him, they would not deal with him, nor would they associate with him or his. This was an early instance in America of what is known now as "boycotting."

It was a very hard thing to be shut out from all dealing and connection with his friends and fellow-citizens, and it was not long before the tea drinker made up his mind that the society and friendship of his neighbors was better even than the highest flavored cup of tea; and so he formally acknowledged his error, begged the pardon of the committee, and promised that thereafter he would act in accordance with their rules and regulations; and his family teapot was put away upon a high top shelf.

But the time came, in a very few years, when the American people attended to their own taxation, and when this teapot, with all the others in the country, could be taken down and freely used without interference with law or conscience.

THE STORY OF A SPY.

WHEN a nation goes to war with another, it is often necessary for the armies on each side to leave behind some of the high and noble principles which may have governed them at home. Of course, war is bloody and cruel, and it almost always happens that the officers and soldiers are obliged to descend also to meanness and duplicity in order to succeed in their campaigns.

One strong reason for this is the necessity for the employment of spies. It is always desirable for the commander of an army to know as far as possible the condition of the enemy's force, and what he is doing or intends to do. Consequently it is a common thing to send spies into the enemy's ranks; and the better those spies can deceive the soldiers of the other side, the more valuable will be their report, if they are fortunate enough to get back into their own camp.

Sometimes a spy will sneak into the enemy's lines, and make his observations in concealment and safety; but the most valuable spies are those which enter an enemy's camp pretending sympathy and friendship. A man who can do this well can find out a great deal.

In every army a spy from the other side is regarded as the worst of enemies, and if captured, his punishment is death. An impartial outsider might object to this severity, when it is considered that the army which punishes the spy may, at the same time, have spies of its own among the enemy. During the Revolution, Major André was executed because he came into the American lines as a spy, and at the same time General Washington was very glad to get a good spy to send into a British camp.

There was a man named John Honeyman, who acted with great success in this capacity on the patriotic side during the Revolution. Honeyman was a Scotch-Irishman, and was said to be a remarkably fine looking man. He was tall, strong, extremely active, and had a fine military bearing. He had no desire to become a soldier; but he was forced into the British army, and came to this country in 1758, when Abercrombie came over to attack the French in Canada. Young Colonel Wolfe, who was afterwards the famous General Wolfe who fell at Quebec, had command of this army, and on the ship in which he sailed was John Honeyman.

Military men are not as sure-footed as sailors on board a ship, which may be rolling and tossing on rough waters; and one day, as Colonel Wolfe was coming into the cabin, he tripped and fell when he was halfway down the companion way, and would probably have broken his neck, if it had not been that Honeyman happened to be at the bottom of the steps, and caught the colonel in his arms, thus saving him from injury.

It is very satisfactory for a full-grown man, especially one whose profession exposes him to accidents of various kinds, to be able to take into his service another man who is tall enough and strong enough to pick him up and carry him if it is necessary, and who is also quick-witted enough to know when he should interpose himself in case of danger.

Honeyman's conduct on this occasion made an impression on Colonel Wolfe; and when afterwards he was made general, he took the tall soldier into his bodyguard, and made him understand that, in times when danger might be apprehended, he was to be as near him as his duties would permit.

When the great attack was made upon Quebec, Honeyman was one of the men who helped row the boat which carried Wolfe over the river; and during this passage a cannon ball from the enemy struck an officer sitting very near Honeyman, and took off his head. Had this happened to Honeyman, it would have been a bad thing for New Jersey.

When they reached the opposite side, Honeyman climbed the Heights of Abraham side by side with his brave commander; and when, in the battle which followed, Wolfe was killed, it was Honeyman who bore him off the field. Thus the first and the last service which this strong man rendered to his military chief were very much the same.

About a year after this the war ended, and Honeyman received an honorable discharge. He carried with him the good will and commendation of his officers, but he also took something which he valued more than these. While he was with General Wolfe, that officer had given him letters expressing his good opinion of him, and these afterwards proved of great service.

Honeyman went southward, and lived for some years in the American Colonies. He finally settled in Philadelphia, where he married. When the Revolution broke out, his sympathies were entirely with the American side, but he did not immediately enlist in the American army. When Washington came to Philadelphia, Honeyman was very anxious to see him and consult with him. It was difficult for a man in the ordinary walks of life to obtain an interview with the commander in chief; but Honeyman sent in the letters which General Wolfe had given him, and, after having read these, Washington was very ready to see the man of whom that general had such a high opinion. Washington soon discovered that Honeyman was a man of peculiar ability, and he had several interviews with him, although it is not known what was said at these times.

Before very long, Honeyman took his family to Griggstown, in Somerset County, New Jersey, and there he hired a house and settled. From this place he went to Fort Lee, when Washington came into New Jersey with his army, and had an interview with the general; and here, it is said, he made a regular contract with the commander in chief to become a spy on the American side.

There were a good many Tories in the State, and,

as Honeyman had once been a British soldier, it was easy enough for him to make believe that he was a Tory, and so make friends with the Redcoats when he should have an opportunity.

The plan concocted between Washington and Honeyman was very carefully worked out in all its details. Honeyman was to let it be known that he was a Tory, and as soon as he thought it proper he was to leave his family and join the British. It was considered that the best thing he could do would be to engage in business as a butcher, and then, when he went over to the British, he could go about the country in search of cattle, and thus get a good idea of what was going on.

He was to stay with the enemy until he discovered something important, and then he was to arrange matters so that he should, apparently without knowing it, wander near the American lines, where he would be captured. It is said that Washington arranged, that, as soon as he should hear that Honeyman had gone over to the enemy, he would offer a reward for his arrest; but this reward would be paid only in case the supposed traitor should be carried alive and unhurt to him. All this planning was necessary, because there was so much communication between the Tories and Whigs at that time, that, if it had been known on the American side that Honeyman had gone over as a spy, the fact would soon have been communicated to the British.

Honeyman went over to the enemy, and started business as a butcher for the army, and, after having gone

a good deal about the country looking for cattle, he
came to New Brunswick with the British army. Nobody had suspected that he was not a perfectly honest
Tory, and he had been paying great attention to the
condition of the British army, and to finding out everything which might be of use if reported to Washington. Among other things, he discovered that the
British forces then occupying Trenton were not under
a strict state of discipline. It was winter; the weather
was cold; apparently there was not much for them to
do; and discipline was in a rather lax state. Honeyman
well understood the habits of the Redcoats, and he
knew that during the holidays the soldiers would live
in even a more free and easy manner than they were
living then.

Not only did he make himself well acquainted with
the condition of the army, but he carefully studied
the town of Trenton and its neighborhood, and, going
about in every direction after cows and oxen, he learned
the roads so well that he could make a very good map
of them. Everything that could be of service to the
American cause was jotted down in Honeyman's re-
tentive memory; and when he had found out everything that he could find out, he thought it was fully
time that he should acquaint Washington with the state
of affairs in the enemy's lines.

He knew that there were American pickets on the
Jersey side, some distance away; and he started out
in this direction as a greasy butcher, with a rope in
one hand and a long whip in the other, looking for
all the world like John Honeyman the Tory cattle-

man, who, if he knew what was good for him, would better keep out of sight of the soldiers of the American army. He walked a long distance down the river, and, though he may have seen cattle, he paid no attention to them. His present object was not to capture anything and take it 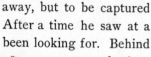 away, but to be captured and taken away. After a time he saw at a distance what he had been looking for. Behind

some bushes, but still quite plain to the eye of this practiced soldier, were two cavalrymen dismounted, and H o n e y m a n knew that they were Americans. He continued to walk towards them until he came close to the spot where the two soldiers were standing.

The moment their eyes fell upon him, they recognized him, and shouted to him to halt; but Honeyman was too good an actor to do that. If he wished to carry on the business in hand, he must keep up his character as a Tory, and so he took to his long legs and ran like a deer. But the men jumped on their horses and were after him in a moment; and as horses' legs are a good deal better than human legs, no matter how long they may be, the flying butcher was soon overtaken. But even then he did not surrender, but so laid about him with his whip that he kept the two men at bay. Of course, if they had not known him, they would have shot him down; but as Washington had issued a proclamation concerning him, and had especially insisted that he should be brought in alive, they did not wish to injure him. But the unequal fight did not continue long, and Honeyman was soon captured. The soldiers bound his arms, and, mounting him behind one of them, so carried him across the river to Washington's camp.

When Honeyman was brought into the presence of the commander in chief, he pretended to be very much frightened; and he would have been excusable if he had been really frightened, for in that little performance of his he had run a great many risks. After asking a few questions of this pretended traitor Washington told the guards to withdraw, and he had a private conference which lasted over half an hour; and in that time it is probable that these two men did a great deal of talking. The information given was most valuable, and such as could have been furnished only by a man of extraordinary powers of observation.

When he had kept Honeyman as long as was necessary, Washington called the guards, and told them to take the prisoner to a log cabin which was used as a military jail, and there to watch him carefully during the night, and in the morning he would

be tried by court-martial. Honeyman was taken to
the prison, which had but one window and one door,
and supper was given to him. He was locked in,
and two sentinels went on guard outside the walls of
the log house.

In the middle of the night these men saw a fire
burning not far from headquarters, and, fearing that
it might prove dangerous to allow it to burn, they
thought it their duty to run and put it out. This
they did, and returned to the log house, where everything looked the same as they had left it. But in
the morning, when they opened the door, there was
no prisoner inside.

It is said that the whole plan of this escape, probably by means of the window, was arranged by
Washington himself, but of this we are not certain.
We know, however, that Washington looked upon
Honeyman as one of the most valuable men in the
employ of the army, and that he would take every
means to prevent him from coming to harm on account of this service.

It was in consequence of the information that
Honeyman, at the cost of such great risk and danger,
had brought to Washington, that three days afterwards
the Americans crossed the Delaware, attacked Trenton, routed the British, and thus gained one of the
greatest and most important victories of the Revolution. If it had been John Honeyman, instead of the
British officer, who was struck by a cannon ball
crossing the St. Lawrence, it is likely that Washington would not have dared to attack the British army

in Trenton, which, before his half hour's conversation with his spy, was believed to be entirely too strong to be meddled with by the Continental soldiers on the other side of the river.

But the report which Honeyman had made to Washington was not the only service which he did to the American cause. Having left his peace principles at home, as he was bound to do if he wanted to act as a truly serviceable spy, he had more work before him. As soon as he got out of the log house, he ran from the camp, and, although he was fired at by a sentinel, he got safely away. He crossed the river on the ice whenever there was any, and when he came to open water, he jumped in and swam, and so he got safely over into the British lines.

There, wet and shivering, he demanded to be taken to the commander; and to him he told the dreadful story of how he had been captured by the American soldiers while he was looking for beef cattle, and how he had been taken to headquarters, questioned, and afterwards shut up in prison, to be shot in the morning, and how he had quietly escaped and come back to his friends. Colonel Rahl, who was in command of the British, was delighted to get hold of this Tory butcher who had been taken prisoner by the Continentals, and he put him through a course of examination about the condition of the enemy.

Of course, it was to the benefit of the Americans that the British should think their army as small and as weak as possible; and so Honeyman gave an account of the wretched condition of the American soldiers, — how few they were, how badly they were armed, how miserably they were officered, and how they were half starved and discouraged. He told this story so well, that he made the colonel laugh, and declare that there was no reason to apprehend any danger from such a pack of ragamuffins as were collected together under Washington, and that, if anybody wished to keep Christmas in a jolly way in his camp, there was no reason why he should not do so.

When Honeyman had finished telling his tales, one to one army and another to the other, he knew that it would be better for him to get out of the neighborhood. He was quite sure that Washington would take Trenton, and, if he should be found in that city when it was captured, it might be hard for even the commander in chief to prevent him from being shot. So he hastened away to take refuge with the British in New Brunswick.

Honeyman had made himself so conspicuous in that part of the country as a Tory who was working as hard as he could for the benefit of the British by supplying them with beef, that all news about him was received with great interest. It was not long before this story of how he had been captured by the American pickets, and afterwards escaped from the log prison, became generally known; and the people of Griggstown, where his wife and family lived, were greatly excited, believing that Honeyman had come there, and had concealed himself in his house. A mob collected in the neighborhood late one night, surrounded the house, and woke up the family with shouts and banging on the door. Mrs. Honeyman appeared, nearly frightened to death; and some of the ringleaders told her that they knew that her Tory husband had come back, and was concealed inside; and they vowed, that, if he did not come out and deliver himself up, they would burn the house and everything in it.

She declared that he was not there, and that it had been a long time since she had seen him. But this was of no use. They persisted that he was inside, and that, if he did not come out very quickly, they would set fire to the house. It was of no use to reason with an excited mob, and, although Mrs. Honeyman said that they might come in and search the house for her husband, they would not listen to her. Perhaps one reason of this was, that Honeyman was a dangerous man to look for, inside of his own house and in dark rooms. Mrs. Honeyman saw that she must act quickly, or her home would be lost to her.

She ran inside, and soon appeared with a paper, which she gave to a man in the crowd with whom she was acquainted, and asked him to read it so that every one could hear.

It was not to be supposed that Mrs. Honeyman possessed a private riot act, which might be read in order to disperse a disorderly assembly; but even the most disorderly people are generally possessed of great curiosity in regard to anything out of the common, and they consented to put off the bonfire a few minutes, and hear what was to be read. What the angry crowd heard was as follows: —

AMERICAN CAMP, NEW JERSEY, 1776.

To the good people of New Jersey, and all others whom it may concern: It is hereby ordered that the wife and children of John Honeyman of Griggstown, the notorious Tory, now within the British lines and probably acting the part of a spy, shall be, and are hereby protected from all harm and annoyance from every quarter until further orders. But this furnishes no protection to Honeyman himself.

GEO. WASHINGTON,
Com.-in-Chief.

This paper, which it is said Washington not only signed, but wrote with his own hand, had been given to Honeyman some time before, and he sent it to his wife in order that it might protect her in case of danger such as now threatened her. It was thought very likely that the people of Griggstown would become so incensed against the Tory butcher, that they might offer harm to his wife and family; and Washington was, no doubt, glad to give what protection he could to the home of the man who, no matter how much he might have deceived other people, was always true to him and to the American cause.

When the crowd heard the communication from the commander in chief of the American army, ordering them to refrain from violence to Mrs. Honeyman and her family, they could not understand why it had been written; but they understood very well what it commanded, and so, grumbling a good deal, but not daring to disobey, they dispersed, and left the wife of the spy in peace.

This paper, of course, was cherished as a great prize by the Honeyman family, and remained in their possession for many years; and it was indeed an heirloom worth preserving. But, although it proved a safeguard for Mrs. Honeyman, it did not remove the prejudices against her husband, and for a long time after that it would have been a very unwise thing for Tory Honeyman to come to Griggstown. Of course, it would have been an easy thing for Washington to have publicly exonerated Honeyman from all charges of treason and Toryism, but this would not have served his purpose. There was still need of a competent spy in the British lines; and there Honeyman remained during the rest of the war, always ready to give information to the commander whenever he could obtain it.

When peace was proclaimed, Washington did not forget Honeyman, and he himself told the story of how this brave man became a Tory butcher for the sake of American independence, and of the great services he had rendered to the cause. Then, of course, Honeyman went home to his wife and family, and the people of Griggstown received him as if he had been a great hero. And in fact, looking at the matter from a war point of view, he deserved all the honors they could give him, for without his aid the battle of Trenton could never have been won; and in fact he was more useful in that engagement than if he had been a regiment of soldiers.

Honeyman was no doubt a great man in Griggstown. The people who had once threatened to burn down his house could not do enough for him. Those who once would not speak to his wife when they met her, now implored her to let them know what they could do for her, and it was not long before the popularity of the family increased to a wonderful degree.

Several officers of rank who had heard of what Honeyman had done, came to see and talk with him; and, more than that, Washington himself came to Griggstown, and paid a visit to his former spy. Such an honor was enough to make the once denounced Tory butcher the leading citizen of the town. Honeyman now became a prosperous man, and bought a large farm and reared a family of seven children, who grew up and prospered; and their descendants are now scattered all over the State. He himself lived to the good old age of ninety-five, and died respected and honored by all, — never thought of as a spy, but only as a patriotic hero.

It would appear, from the stories of those early days, that whenever a man or woman acted a good part, and was truly of service to New Jersey, he or she always lived to be very old, and left behind a vast number of descendants.

A MAN WHO COVETED WASHINGTON'S SHOES.

THE person whose story we are now about to tell was not a Jerseyman; but, as most of the incidents which make him interesting to us occurred in this State, we will give him the benefit of a few years' residence here.

This was General Charles Lee, who might well have been called a soldier of fortune. He was born in England, but the British Isles were entirely too small to satisfy his wild ambitions and his roving disposition. There are few heroes of romance who have had such a wide and varied experience, and who have engaged in so many strange enterprises. He was a brave man and very able, but he had a fault which prevented him from being a high-class soldier; and that fault was, that he could not bear restraint, and was always restive under command of another, and, while always ready to tell other people what they ought to do, was never willing to be told what he ought to do.

He joined the British army when he was a young man; and he first came to this country in 1757, when General Abercrombie brought over an army to fight the French. For three years, Lee was engaged in the wilds and forests, doing battle with the Indians and the French, and no doubt he had all the adventures an ordinary person would desire. But this experience was far from satisfactory.

When he left America, he went to Portugal with another British army, and there he fought the Spanish with as much impetuosity as he had fought the French and Indians.

Life was absolutely tasteless to Lee without a very strong sprinkle of variety. Consequently he now tried fighting in an entirely different field, and went into politics. He became a Liberal, and with his voice fought the government for whom he had been previously fighting with his sword.

But a few years of this satisfied him; and then he went to Poland, where he became a member of the king's staff, and as a Polish officer disported himself for two years.

It is very likely that in Turkey a high-spirited man would find more opportunities for lively adventure than even in Poland. At any rate, Charles Lee thought so; and to Turkey he went, and entered into the service of the Sultan. Here he distinguished himself in a company of Turks who were guarding a great treasure in its transportation from Moldavia to Constantinople. No doubt he wore a turban and baggy trousers, and carried a great scimiter, for a man of that sort is not likely to do things by halves when he does them at all.

Having had such peculiar experiences in various armies and various parts of the world, Lee thought himself qualified to occupy a position of rank in the British army, and, coming back to England, he endeavored to obtain military promotion. But the government there did not seem to think he had learned enough in Poland and Turkey to enable him to take precedence of English officers accustomed to command English troops, and it declined to put him above such officers, and to give him the place he desired. Lee was not a man of mild temper. He became very angry at the treatment he received, and, abandoning his native country again, he went to Russia, where the Czar gave him the command of a company of wild Cossacks. But he did not remain long with the Cossacks. Perhaps they were not wild and daring enough to suit his fancy, although there are very few fancies which would not be satisfied with the reckless and furious demeanor generally attributed to these savage horsemen.

He threw up his command and went to Hungary, and there he did some fighting in an entirely different fashion. Not having any opportunity to distinguish himself upon a battlefield, he engaged in a duel; and of course, as he was acting the part of a hero of romance, he killed his man.

Hungary was not a suitable residence for him after the duel, and he went back to England, and there he found the country in a state of excitement in regard to the American Colonies. Now, if there was anything that Lee liked, it was a state of excitement, and in the midst of this political hubbub he felt.as much at home as if he had been charging the ranks of an enemy. Of course, he took part against the government, for, as far as we know, he had always been against it, and he became a violent supporter of the rights of the colonists.

He was so much in earnest in this matter, that in 1773 he came to America to see for himself how matters stood. When he got over here, he became more strongly in favor of the colonists than he had been at home, and everywhere proclaimed that the Americans were right in resisting the unjust taxation claims of Great Britain. As he had always been ready to lay aside his British birthright and become some sort of a foreigner, he now determined to become an American; and to show that he was in earnest, he went down to Virginia and bought a farm there.

Lee soon became acquainted with people in high places in American politics; and when the first Congress assembled, he was ready to talk with its members, urging them to stand up for their rights, and draw their swords and load their guns in defense of independence. It was quite natural, that, when the Revolution really began, a man who was so strongly in favor of the patriots, and had had so much military experience in so many different lands, should be allowed to take part in the war, and Charles Lee was appointed major general.

This was a high military position, — much higher, in fact, than he could ever have obtained in his own country, — but it did not satisfy him. The position he wanted was that of commander in chief of the American army; and he was surprised and angry that it was not offered to him, and that a man of his ability should be passed over, and that high place given to a person like George Washington, who knew but little of war, and had no idea whatever how the thing was done in Portugal, Poland, Russia, and Turkey, and who was, in fact, no more than a country gentleman.

All this showed that these Americans were fools, who did not understand their best interests. But as there was a good chance for a fight, and, in fact, a good many fights, and as a major-generalship was not to be sneered at, he accepted it, and resigned the commission which he held in the English army.

He was doubtless in earnest in his desire to assist the Americans to obtain their independence, for he was always in earnest when he was doing anything that he was inclined to do. But he did not propose to sacrifice his own interests to the cause he had undertaken; and as, by entering the American army, he risked the loss of his estate in England, he arranged with Congress for compensation for such loss.

But, although General Lee was now a very ardent American soldier, he could not forgive Mr. Washington for taking command above him. If that Virginia gentleman had had the courtesy and good sense which were generally attributed to him, he would have resigned the supreme command, and, modestly stepping aside, would have asked General Lee to accept it. At least, that was the opinion of General Charles Lee.

As this high and mighty soldier was so unwilling to submit to the orders of incompetent people, he never liked to be under the direct command of Washington, and, if it were possible to do so, he managed to be concerned in operations not under the immediate eye of the commander in chief. In fact, he was very jealous indeed of Washington, and did not hesitate to express his opinion about him whenever he had a chance.

The American army was not very successful in Long Island, and there was a time when it fared very badly in New Jersey; and Lee was not slow to declare that these misfortunes were owing entirely to the ignorance of the man who was in command. Moreover, if there was any one who wanted to know if there was another man in the Colonies who could command the army better, and lead it more certainly and speedily to victory, General Lee was always ready to mention an experienced soldier who would be able to perform that duty most admirably.

If it had not been for this unfortunate and jealous disposition, Charles Lee — a very different man from "Light Horse Harry" Lee — would have been one of the most useful officers in the American army. But he had such a jealousy of Washington, and hoped so continually that something would happen which would give him the place then occupied by the Virginia country gentleman, that, although he was at heart an honest patriot, he allowed himself to do things which were not at all patriotic. He wanted to see the Americans successful in the country, but he did not want to see all that happen under the leadership of Washington; and if he could put an obstacle in the way of that incompetent person, he would do it, and be glad to see him stumble over it.

In the winter of 1776, when the American army was making its way across New Jersey, towards the Delaware River; with Cornwallis in pursuit, Washington was anxiously looking for the troops, under the command of General Lee, who had been ordered to come to his assistance; and if ever assistance was needed, it was needed then. But Lee liked to do his own ordering, and, instead of hurrying to help Washington, he thought it would be a great deal better to do something on his own account; and so he endeavored to get into the rear of Cornwallis's army, thinking, that, if he should attack the enemy in that way, he might possibly win a startling victory, which would cover him with glory, and show how much better a soldier he was than that poor Washington who was retreating across the country, instead of boldly turning and showing fight.

If Lee had been a true soldier, and had conscientiously obeyed the commands of his superior, he would have joined Washington and his army without delay, and a short time afterward would have had an opportunity of taking part in the battle of Trenton, in which the Virginia country gentleman defeated the British, and gained one of the most important victories of the war.

Lee pressed slowly onward — ready to strike a great blow for himself, and unwilling to help anybody else strike a blow — until he came to Morristown; and, after staying there one night, he proceeded in the direction of Basking Ridge, a pretty village not far away. Lee left his army at Bernardsville, which was then known as Vealtown, and rode on to Basking Ridge, accompanied only by a small guard. There he took lodgings at an inn, and made himself comfortable. The next morning he did not go and put himself at the head of his army and move on, because there were various affairs which occupied his attention.

Several of his guard wished to speak to him, some of them being men from Connecticut, who appeared before him in full-bottomed wigs, showing plainly that they considered themselves people who were important enough to have their complaints attended to. One of them wanted his horse shod, another asked for some money on account of his pay, and a third had something to say about rations. But General Lee cut them all off very shortly with, "You want a great deal, but you have not mentioned what you want most. You want to go home, and I should be glad to let you go, for you are no good here." Then his adjutant general asked to see him; and he had a visit from a Major Wilkinson, who arrived that morning with a letter from General Gates.

All these things occupied him very much, and he did not sit down to breakfast till ten o'clock. Shortly after they had finished .their meal, and Lee was writing a letter to General Gates, in which he expressed a very contemptible opinion of General Washington, Major Wilkinson saw, at the end of the lane which led from the house down to the main road, a party of British cavalry, who dashed round the corner toward the house. The major immediately called out to General Lee that the Redcoats were coming; but Lee, who was a man not to be frightened by sudden reports, finished signing the letter, and then jumped up to see what was the matter.

By this time the dragoons had surrounded the house; and when he perceived this, General Lee naturally wanted to know where the guards were, and why they did not fire on these fellows. But there was no firing, and apparently there were no guards; and when Wilkinson went to look for them, he found their arms in the room which had been their quarters, but the men were gone. These private soldiers had evidently been quite as free and easy, and as bent upon making themselves comfortable, as had been the general, and they had had no thought that such a thing as a British soldier was anywhere in the neighborhood. When Wilkinson looked out of the door, he saw the guards running in every direction, with dragoons chasing them.

What all this meant, nobody knew at first; and Wilkinson supposed that it was merely a band of marauders of the British army, who were making a raid into the country to get what they could in the way of plunder. It was not long before this was found to be a great mistake; for the officer in command of the dragoons called from the outside, and demanded that General Lee should surrender himself, and that, if he did not do so in five minutes, the house would be set on fire.

Now, it was plain to everybody that the British had heard of the leisurely advance of this American general, and that he had left his command and come to Basking Ridge to take his ease at an inn, and so they had sent a detachment to capture him. Soon the women of the house came to General Lee, and urged him to hide himself under a feather bed. They declared that they would cover him up so that nobody would suspect that he was in the bed; then they would tell the soldiers that he was not there, and that they might come and search the house if they chose.

But although Lee was a jealous man and a hasty man, he had a soul above such behavior as this, and would not hide himself in a feather bed; but, as there was no honorable way of escape, he boldly came forward and surrendered himself.

The British gave him no time to make any preparations for departure. They did not know but that his army might be on the way to Basking Ridge; and the sooner they were off, the better. So they made him jump on Major Wilkinson's horse, which was tied by the door; and in his slippers and dressing gown, and without a hat, this bold soldier of wide experience, who thought he should be commander in chief of the American army, was hurried away at full gallop. He was taken to New York, where he was put into prison. It is said that Lee plotted against America during his imprisonment; but General Washington did not know that, and used every exertion to have him exchanged, so that his aspiring rival soon again joined the American army.

But his misfortune had no good effect upon General Charles Lee, who came back to his command with as high an opinion of himself, and as low an opinion of certain other people, as he had had when he involuntarily left it. It was some time after this, at the battle of Monmouth Court House, that Charles Lee showed what sort of a man he really was. He had now become so jealous that he positively determined that he would not obey orders, and would act as he thought best. He had command of a body of troops numbering five thousand, a good-sized army for those days, and he was ordered to advance to Monmouth Court House and attack the enemy who were there, while Washington, with another force, would hasten to his assistance as rapidly as possible.

Washington carried out his part of the plan; but when he had nearly reached Monmouth, he found, to his amazement, that Lee had gone there, but had done no fighting at all, and was now actually retreating, and coming in his direction. As it would be demoralizing in the highest degree to his own command, if Lee's armed forces in full retreat should come upon them, Washington hurried forward to prevent anything of the sort, and soon met Lee. When the latter was asked what was the meaning of this strange proceeding, he could give no good reason, except that he thought it better not to risk an engagement at that time.

Then the Virginia country gentleman blazed out at the soldier of fortune, and it is said that no one ever heard George Washington speak to any other man as he spoke to General Lee on that day. He was told to go back to his command and to obey orders, and together the American forces moved on. In the battle which followed, the enemy was repulsed; but the victory was not so complete as it should have been, for the British departed in the night and went where they intended to go, without being cut off by the American army, as would have been the case if Lee had obeyed the orders which were given him.

General Lee was very angry at the charges which Washington had made against him, and demanded that he should be tried by court-martial. His wish was granted. He was tried, and found guilty of every charge made against him, and in consequence was suspended from the army for one year.

But Charles Lee never went back into the American army. Perhaps he had had enough of it. In any event, it had had enough of him; and seven years afterwards, when he died of a fever, his ambition to stand in Washington's shoes died with him. While he lived on his Virginia farm, he was as impetuous and eccentric as when he had been in the army, and he must have been a very unpleasant neighbor. In fact, the people there thought he was crazy. This opinion was not changed when his will was read, for in that document he said, —

"I desire most earnestly that I may not be buried in any church or churchyard, or within a mile of any Presbyterian or Anabaptist meetinghouse; for since I have resided in this country I have kept so much bad company when living, that I do not choose to continue it when dead."

THE MAN IN THE "AUGER HOLE."

WHEN we consider the American Revolution, we are apt to think of it as a great war in which all the inhabitants of the Colonies rose up against Great Britain, determined, no matter what might be the hardships and privations, no matter what the cost in blood and money, to achieve their independence and the right to govern themselves.

But this was not the case. A great majority of the people of the Colonies were ardently in favor of independence; but there were also a great many people, and we have no right to say that some of them were not very good people, who were as well satisfied that their country should be a colony of Great Britain as the Canadians are now satisfied with that state of things, and who were earnestly and honestly opposed to any separation from the mother country.

This difference of opinion was the cause of great trouble and bloodshed among the colonists themselves, and the contests between the Tories and the Whigs were nowhere more bitter than in New Jersey. In some parts of the Colony, families were divided against themselves; and not only did this result in quarrels and separations, but fathers and sons, and brothers and brothers, fought against each other. At one time the Tories, or, as they came to be called, "refugees," were in such numbers that they took possession of the town of Freehold, and held it for more than a week; and when at last the town was retaken by the patriotic forces, most of them being neighbors and friends of the refugees, several prominent Tories were hanged, and many others sent to prison.

The feeling between the Americans of the two different parties was more violent than that between the patriots and the British troops, and before long it became entirely unsafe for any Tory to remain in his own home in New Jersey. Many of them went to New York, where the patriotic feeling was not so strong at that time, and there they formed themselves into a regular military company called the "Associated Loyalists;" and this company was commanded by William Temple Franklin, son of the great Benjamin Franklin, who had been appointed governor of New Jersey by the British Crown. He was now regarded with great hatred by the patriots of New Jersey, because he was a strong Tory. This difference of opinion between William Franklin and his father was the most noted instance of this state of feeling which occurred in those days.

It will be interesting to look upon this great contest from a different point of view than that from which we are accustomed to regard it; and some extracts from the journal of a New Jersey lady who was a decided Tory, will give us an idea of the feeling and condition of the people who were opposed to the Revolution.

This lady was Mrs. Margaret Hill Morris, who lived in Burlington. She was a Quaker lady, and must have been a person of considerable wealth; for she had purchased the house on Green Bank, one of the prettiest parts of Burlington, overlooking the river, in which Governor Franklin had formerly resided. This was a fine house, and contained the room which afterwards became celebrated under the name of the "Auger Hole." This had been built, for what reason is not known, as a place of concealment. It was a small room, entirely dark, but said to be otherwise quite comfortable, which could be approached only through a linen closet. In order to get at it, the linen had to be taken from the shelves, the shelves drawn out, and a small door opened at the back of the closet, quite low down, so that the dark room could only be entered by stooping.

In this "auger hole," Mrs. Morris, who was a strong Tory, but a very good woman, had concealed a refugee who at the time was sought for by the adherents of the patriotic side, and who probably would have had a hard time of it if he had been caught, for he was a person of considerable importance.

The name of the refugee was Jonathan Odell, and he was rector of St. Mary's Church in Burlington. He was a learned man, being a doctor as well as a clergyman and a very strong Tory. He had been of much service to the people of Burlington; for when the Hessians had attacked the town, he had come forward and interceded with their commander, and had done his work so well that the soldiers were forbidden to pillage the town. But when the Hessians

left, the American authorities began a vigorous search
for Tories; and Parson Odell was obliged to conceal
himself in good Mrs. Morris's "auger hole."

Mrs. Morris was apparently a widow who lived
alone with her two boys, and, having this refugee in
her house, she was naturally very nervous about the
movements of the American troops and the actions
of her neighbors of the opposite party.

She kept a journal of the things that happened
about her in those eventful days, and from this we
will give some extracts. It must be understood that
in writing her journal, the people designated as the
"enemy" were the soldiers under Washington, and
that "gondolas" were American gunboats.

"From the 13th to the 16th we had various reports of the advancing and retiring of the enemy; parties of armed men rudely
entered the town and diligent search was made for tories. Some of
the gondola gentry broke into and pillaged Rd Smith's house on
the bank. About noon this day [16th] a very terrible account of
thousands coming into the town, and now actually to be seen on
Gallows Hill: my incautious son caught up the spyglass, and was
running towards the mill to look at them. I told him it would be
liable to misconstruction."

The journal states that the boy went out with the
spyglass, but could get no good place from which he
could see Gallows Hill, or any troops upon it, and
so went down to the river, and thought he would take
a view of the boats in which were the American
troops. He rested his spyglass on the low limb of
a tree, and with a boyish curiosity inspected the
various boats of the little fleet, not suspecting that
any one would object to such a harmless proceeding.

But the people on the boats saw him, and did object very much; and the consequence was, that, not long after he reached his mother's house, a small boat from one of the vessels came to shore. A party of men went to the front door of the house in which they had seen the boy enter, and began loudly to knock upon it. Poor Mrs. Morris was half frightened to death, and she made as much delay as possible in order to compose her features and act as if she had never heard of a refugee who wished to hide himself from his pursuers. In the mild manner in which Quaker women are always supposed to speak, she asked them what they wanted. They quickly told her that they had heard that there was a refugee, to whom they applied some very strong language, who was hiding somewhere about here, and that they had seen him spying at them with a glass from behind a tree, and afterwards watched him as he entered this house.

Mrs. Morris declared that they were entirely mistaken; that the person they had seen was no one but her son, who had gone out to look at them as any boy might do, and who was perfectly innocent of any designs against them. The men may have been satisfied with this explanation in regard to her son; but they asserted that they knew that there was a refugee concealed somewhere in that neighborhood, and they believed that he was in an empty house near by, of which they were told she had the key. Mrs. Morris, who had given a signal, previously agreed upon, to the man in the "auger hole," to keep very quiet, wished to gain as much time as possible, and exclaimed,

"Bless me! I hope you are not Hessians."

"Do we look like Hessians?" asked one of them rudely.

"Indeed, I don't know."

"Did you ever see a Hessian?"

"No, never in my life; but they are men, and you are men, and may be Hessians, for anything I know. But I will go with you into Colonel Cox's house, though indeed it was my son at the mill; he is but a boy, and meant no harm; he wanted to see the troops."

So she took the key of the empty house referred to, and went in ahead of the men, who searched the place thoroughly, and, after finding no place where anybody could be, they searched one or two of the houses adjoining; but for some reason they did not think it worth while to go through Mrs. Morris's own house. Had they done so, it is not probable that the good lady could have retained her composure, especially if they had entered the room in which was the linen closet; for, even had they been completely deceived by the piles of sheets and pillow-cases, there is no knowing but that the unfortunate man in the "auger hole" might have been inclined to sneeze.

But although she was a brave woman, and very humanely inclined, Mrs. Morris felt she could not any longer take the risk of a refugee in her house. And so that night, after dark, she went up to the parson in the "auger hole," and made him come out; and she took him into the town, where he was concealed by some of the Tory citizens, who were better adapted to take care of the refugee than this lone Quaker woman with her two inquisitive boys. It is believed that soon after this he took refuge in New York, which was then in the hands of the British.

Further on in the journal, Mrs. Morris indulges in some moral reflections in regard to the war in which her countrymen were engaged, and no one of right feeling will object to her sentiments.

"Jan. 14. I hear Gen. Howe sent a request to Washington desiring three days cessation of arms to take care of the wounded and bury the dead, which was refused: what a woeful tendency war has to harden the human heart against the tender feelings of humanity. Well may it be called a *horrid art* thus to change the nature of man. I thought that even barbarous nations had a sort of religious regard for their dead."

After this the journal contains many references to warlike scenes on the river and warlike sounds from the country around. Numbers of gondolas filled with soldiers went up and down the river, at times cannon from distant points firing alarums. At other times the roaring of great guns from a distance, showing that a battle was going on, kept the people of Burlington in a continual excitement; and Mrs. Morris, who was entirely cut off from her relatives and friends, several of whom were living in Philadelphia, was naturally very anxious and disturbed in regard to events, of which she heard but little, and perhaps understood less.

One day she saw a number of gunboats, with flags flying and drums beating, that were going, she was told, to attend a court-martial at which a number of refugees, men of her party, were to be tried by General Putnam; and it was believed that if they were found guilty they would be executed.

After a time, Mrs. Morris found an opportunity of showing, that, although in principle she might be a Tory, she was at heart a good, kind Quaker lady ready to give help to suffering people, no matter whether they belonged to the side she favored or to that which she opposed.

Some of the people who came up the river in the gunboats — and in many cases the soldiers brought their wives with them, probably as cooks — were taken sick during that summer; and some of these invalids stopped at Burlington, being unable to proceed farther.

Here, to their surprise, they found no doctors; for all the patriots of that profession had gone to the army, and the Tory physicians had departed to the British lines. But, as has been said before, the women in the early days of New Jersey were often obliged to be physicians; and among the good housewives of

Burlington, who knew all about herb teas, homemade plasters, and potions, Mrs. Morris held a high position. The sick Continentals were told that she was just as good as a doctor, and, besides, was a very kind woman, always ready to help the sick and suffering.

So some of the sick soldiers came to her; and from what Mrs. Morris wrote, one or two of them must have been the same men who had previously come to her house and threatened the life of her boy, who had been looking at them with a spyglass. But now they very meekly and humbly asked her to come and attend their poor comrades who were unable to move. At first Mrs. Morris thought this was some sort of a trick, and that they wanted to get her on board of one of the gunboats, and carry her away. But when she found that the sick people were in a house in the town, she consented to go and do what she could. So she took her bottles with her, and her boxes and her herbs, and visited the sick people, several of whom she found were women.

They were all afflicted with some sort of a fever, probably of a malarial kind, contracted from living day and night on board of boats without proper protection; and, knowing just what to do in such cases, she, to use her own expression, "treated them according to art," and it was not long before they all recovered.

What happened in consequence of this hospital work for those whom she considered her enemies, is thus related by Mrs. Morris:—

"I thought I had received all my pay when they thankfully acknowledged all my kindness, but lo! in a short time afterwards, a very rough, ill-looking man came to the door and asked for me. When I went to him, he drew me aside and asked me if I had any friends in Philadelphia. The question alarmed me, supposing that there was some mischief meditated against that poor city; however, I calmly said, 'I have an ancient father-in-law, some sisters, and other near friends there.' 'Well,' said the man, 'do you wish to hear from them, or send anything by way of refreshment to them? If you do, I will take charge of it and bring you back anything you may send for.' I was very much surprised, to be sure, and thought he only wanted to get provisions to take to the gondolas, when he told me his wife was one I had given medicine to, and this was the only thing he could do to pay me for my kindness. My heart leaped for joy, and I set about preparing something for my dear absent friends. A quarter of beef, some veal, fowls, and flour, were soon put up, and about midnight the man came and took them away in his boat."

Mrs. Morris was not mistaken in trusting to the good intentions of this grateful Continental soldier, for, as she says, two nights later there came a loud knocking at the door:—

"Opening the chamber window, we heard a man's voice saying, 'Come down softly and open the door, but bring no light.' There was something mysterious in such a call, and we concluded to go down and set the candle in the kitchen. When we got to the front door we asked, 'Who are you?' The man replied, 'A friend;

open quickly: ' so the door was opened, and who should it be but our honest gondola man with a letter, a bushel of salt, a jug of molasses, a bag of rice, some tea, coffee, and sugar, and some cloth for a coat for my poor boys — all sent by my kind sisters. How did our hearts and eyes overflow with love to them and thanks to our Heavenly Father for such seasonable supplies. May we never forget it. Being now so rich, we thought it our duty to hand out a little to the poor around us, who were mourning for want of salt, so we divided the bushel and gave a pint to every poor person who came for it, and had a great plenty for our own use."

As the war drew to its close and it became plain to every one that the cause of the patriots must triumph, the feeling between the two parties of Americans became less bitter; and the Tories, in many cases, saw that it would be wise for them to accept the situation, and become loyal citizens of the United States of America, as before they had been loyal subjects of Great Britain.

When peace was at last proclaimed, those Tories who were prisoners were released, and almost all of them who had owned farms or estates had them returned to them, and Mrs. Morris could visit her "ancient father-in-law" and her sisters in Philadelphia, or they could come up the river and visit her in her house on the beautiful Green Bank at Burlington, without fear or thought of those fellow-countrymen who had been their bitter enemies.

THE STORY OF TWO CAPTAINS.

DURING the Revolution, New Jersey had a very hard time, harder in some ways than many of her sister States. This may be accounted for by the fact that much of her territory lay between the two important cities of Philadelphia and New York, and that it was therefore liable to be the scene of frequent battles and marches. In fact, it often happens that the march of an enemy through a quiet country is almost as bad as a disastrous battle.

Country people and farmers, especially those of fruitful and prosperous countries, are generally much more opposed to war than people in cities; and so it happened in New Jersey. When the Revolution began, there were a good many people who did not care particularly about taxation, who had been happy and comfortable all their days, without any thought of independence, and who saw no reason why they should not continue to be so; and these did not immediately spring to arms when the first guns of the war were fired. There were no large cities in New Jersey. It was a rural community, a country of peaceable people.

When the British troops first entered New Jersey, and before any battles had been fought, the commander in chief took advantage of this state of feeling, and endeavored as far as possible to make the people think that the Redcoats were in reality good friends, and intended them no harm. He protested, whenever he had a chance, that when these disturbances were over, any complaints that the people had to make in regard to the laws made by their English rulers, should be carefully attended to, and their grievances redressed as soon as possible.

As has been said before, a great many of the people of the Colony were in favor of continuance of the British rule, and from these arose that Tory party which afterwards caused so much bitterness of feeling and bloody contention. But there were also others, who, although they were not Tories, were not in favor of fighting if it could be helped, and these the British commander most wished to conciliate. He issued a great many printed papers of protection, which he gave to those who had not yet taken sides against the Crown. The people who received these were assured, that, so long as they had them to show, no Redcoat soldier would in any way disturb them or their property.

But when the English army actually spread itself over the country, and the soldiers began to forage about to see what they could find to eat and drink better than their rations, the Jersey farmers frequently discovered that these papers of protection were of no use at all. If shown to one of the Hessians, who were more dreaded than the other soldiers of the British army, the German could not read a word of it, and paid no attention to it. He wanted ducks and geese, and took them. And after a time the English soldiers determined that the Hessians should not take all they wanted while they stood by and had nothing, and so they began to pillage, without regard to the little printed papers which the angry farmers showed them.

This state of things had a very good effect upon the rural population of New Jersey; and as the conduct of the British soldiers became more lawless, so did the determination to resist such outrageous actions become stronger and stronger in the hearts of the people of the country, and they readily listened to the calls to arms which were made by Washington and by Congress. The people who were in favor of the Revolution and independence stood together and formed themselves on one side, while those who were still loyal to the King formed themselves on the other. And thus, with both the Tories and the British against them, the citizens of New Jersey began in good earnest to fight for their liberties.

In the war which was now waged in New Jersey, it very often happened that the British soldiers had no part whatever; and although the battles and skirmishes between the Tories and the Whigs were generally small and of no great importance, they were always violent and bloody. Sometimes the forces on each side were considerable enough to entitle the affair to be called a battle. The forces of the Whigs or patriots in these encounters were almost always composed of the militiamen of the State, who had not joined the regular army, but who had enlisted for the purpose of defending their own homes and farms. In various parts of the country there were men who, some on one side and some on the other, had distinguished themselves as soldiers.

One of the most prominent of these was a Captain Huddy of Monmouth County. He had command of a company of militiamen, and he made himself very formidable to the bodies of Tories who had formed themselves in the country, and his name and fame as a great fighter began to spread over that part of the State. He lived in a good-sized house, for that time, in the village of Colt's Neck, and in this house he generally kept part of his command.

But one evening he happened to be at home without any one with him except a servant, a negro girl about twenty years old. His men had all gone away on some errand, and the fact that the captain was at home by himself became known to some Tories in the neighborhood. These, led by a mulatto named Tye, made an attack upon his house.

But although Captain Huddy's men were all away, they had left their guns behind; and so the brave Huddy, instead of surrendering to the force of fifty or sixty Tories who were outside, determined to fight them, with no garrison but himself and the negro girl, and he made ready to hold his house as long as he could. The girl loaded the guns; and Huddy, running from one window to another, fired at the Tories so rapidly and with such good effect, that they believed that there were a number of men in the house, and so did not dare to rush forward and break in the doors, as they certainly would have done if they had known that they were fighting two persons only, and one of them a girl.

Several of the attacking party were wounded, and they found at last that there was little chance of capturing this fortress, so well defended: so they concluded to burn the house, and thus force the garrison to come out. While they were at work setting fire to the wooden building, Huddy shot the mulatto in the arm; but, finding that he could not prevent them from carrying out their purpose, he shouted to them that if they would put out the fire, he would surrender.

When the fort had capitulated and the enemy marched in, the Tories were so angry to find that they had been fighting no one but a man and a negro girl, that many of them were inclined to fall upon these unfortunates, and butcher them on the spot; but they were restrained. As it was known that Huddy's men would probably soon return, — for the noise of the firing had aroused the neighborhood, — the enemy seized the captain and hurried him away, leaving the rest of the garrison behind.

It may be said here that this girl, whose name was Lucretia Emmons, afterwards married a man named Chambers, and, like all other Jersey women who were of benefit to their State, lived to a good old age, and had a large posterity.

Captain Huddy was hurried away to the boats in which the Tories had arrived; but the militiamen were in hot pursuit, and a running fight took place between them and the Tories, in which six of the latter were killed. The Tories, with their prisoner, got on board their boats; but they had not pushed very far from the shore, before the militiamen were firing at them again. During the hubbub which ensued, Captain Huddy made a bold dash for liberty. He sprang to his feet, plunged into the water, and began to swim to the shore. In so doing, unfortunately, he received a shot in the thigh from his own friends; but he raised his hands above his head and shouted, "I am Huddy, I am Huddy!" and so, with one leg and two arms, he continued to strike out for the shore, which he reached in safety. His wound could not have been very severe, for it was not long before he was again engaged in fighting the Tories.

Two years after this, Captain Huddy was once more obliged to hold a fort against a superior body of Tories, — this time a rude structure of logs, or blockhouse, near Tom's River, close to the coast. His garrison consisted of twenty-five men. Here he was attacked by a number of refugees, some of them from New York, and some from the neighborhood. They gathered from various quarters during the night, and early on a Sunday morning they made a united attack on the blockhouse. Huddy and his men fought bravely; but when their ammunition was gone, and seven or eight of them were killed, he was obliged to surrender.

Now, there was no one to rescue him, and he was marched away, put in irons, and confined in the hold of a prison ship anchored off the coast. The state of feeling at the time is shown by the way in which the commander of this expedition speaks of the village of Tom's River; for he says, "The Town, as it is called, consists of about a dozen houses, in which none but a piratical set of banditti reside."

What afterwards happened to the captain was the result of a chain of events which could only have occurred in a country where neighbors and former friends were arrayed in bloody conflict against each

other. A prominent Tory of that neighborhood, named
White, had been captured by the patriots, and it happened that the father of one of White's guards had
been murdered by a party of Tories of whom White
was a member. White was shot soon after his capture; and it was generally believed that he had been
killed by this guard, who wished to avenge his father's
death.

Thus one murder led to another, but the bloody
business had not yet gone far enough. The friends
of White were determined to avenge his death, and
could think of no better way of doing it than by
killing Captain Huddy. The Tories wished to get
rid of him anyway, and here was a reason which
was considered good enough in those days of furious
animosity between fellow-countrymen. It was not
long, therefore, before Huddy was taken from his
prison, and, without even a show of a trial, was condemned to death. It was said that he assisted in
the killing of White; and although he asserted boldly
that this was an absurd charge, as he was in prison
at the time White was shot, the Tories would not
listen to any such plea. They were determined to
kill him, and die he must.

He was taken on shore at Sandy Hook, and on
the beach a rude gallows was constructed of three
fence rails, and there he was hung. Before he died,
he wrote his will, resting the paper on the top of a
flour barrel; and it is said that his handwriting was
as firm and legible as if he had been sitting at a
table in his own house.

This inhuman and lawless execution of a man so well known and of such good reputation as Captain Huddy, created great indignation in the patriotic party all over the country, and there was a general demand that the British army should deliver up a man named Lippencot, who had been the leader of the party which had hung Huddy; but the British did not consent to this. They did make a show of investigating the matter; and Lippencot, who was an officer of a refugee regiment regularly enlisted in the British service, was tried by court-martial. But he was acquitted; and no satisfaction was offered to the Americans for this crime, which had been committed in open defiance of the laws of war.

But the British commander in chief, who arrived about this time, was a man of honor and good sense, and he openly condemned the action of Lippencot and his men, and assured the Americans that he would do what he could to further investigate the matter.

This, however, did not satisfy the country, and from every side there came demands that some one of the officers who were then prisoners in the American lines should be executed in retaliation for Huddy's murder, unless Lippencot were delivered up to the Americans. Here, then, opened the fourth act of this bloody play of progression, and we will tell the story of the other captain.

It is a horrible thing to deliberately execute an innocent man because some one else has committed a crime; but war is horrible, and we must expect that horrible things will continually spring from it. As no satisfaction could be obtained from the British for this acknowledged outrage and murder, — for in acquitting Lippencot the British authorities virtually took upon themselves the responsibility of Huddy's execution, — the Americans, being at war and acting in accordance with the bloody rules of war, deter-

mined to select an officer from among the English pris- oners in the Amer- ican lines, who should be executed in retaliation for Huddy's death.

As soon as this order had been is- sued, thirteen Brit- ish officers, who were at liberty on parole in the Amer- ican lines, were ordered to report at Lancaster, Penn., in order that one of them might be selected to be the victim of retaliation.

These officers were assembled in a room of the Black Bear Tavern with several American officers, who conducted the proceedings, and a guard of mounted dragoons was stationed outside.

The question was to be decided by lot according to the following plan: the thirteen names of the offi-

cers were written each upon a little slip of paper,
and these were put into a hat. Then in another hat
were placed thirteen other slips of the same size, all
of them blank excepting one, on which was written
the word "unfortunate." Two drummer boys were
called in to draw out the slips, one from one hat,
the other from the other. As one boy drew out the
piece of paper and read the name of the officer
written upon it, the other boy at the same time drew
a slip from the other hat. After several drawings,
in which the slips from the second hat had all been
blank, one of the boys drew, and read upon the little
piece of paper the name of Captain Asgill, and at
the same time the other boy drew out a slip, and
read the word "unfortunate." This decided the matter; and the American officer in command turned to
the leader of the dragoons and said to him, "This
gentleman, sir, is your prisoner."

Now this most tragical meeting broke up, and we
are told that every man in that room, except Captain
Asgill himself, was in tears. The truly unfortunate
man who had been chosen by this most doleful
chance was a handsome young gentleman, scarcely
more than a boy. He was beloved by every one
who knew him, and he would have been the last
man to have consented to any such deed as that for
which he was to pay the penalty. When it became
known that he had been selected by fate to be executed in retaliation, every one who knew anything
about him, either in the British army or the American, deeply deplored the fact that the doom should

have fallen on one who so little deserved it. Captain
Asgill was taken to Philadelphia, and after a while
was carried to New Jersey, where in Chatham, Morris
County, he was held to await his end.

Washington himself was greatly affected by this
event; and he wrote to the colonel who had charge
of Captain Asgill, to treat the unfortunate young
man with all tenderness and respect while he should
be in his hands, and to do everything for him that
was consistent with propriety under the circumstances.

Now, there came from many parts of this country,
as well as from the English, all sorts of communications and memorials addressed to the government and
the commander of the army, urging clemency in the
case of this unfortunate young man; and it was no
doubt in consequence of these, that his punishment
was delayed from time to time.

Captain Asgill's mother was a lady of good position
in England, and, overwhelmed with grief at the impending fate of her son, she spared no efforts to save
him. She wrote to every man of influence whom she
knew; and among others she wrote to the Count de
Vergennes, who was in this country as the representative of the court of France.

The French, who had been the faithful friends of
the Americans throughout the struggle, were as willing to assist their allies to be merciful and forgiving
as they were to help them fight their battles. The
ambassador addressed a strong letter to Congress,
urging that young Captain Asgill might be spared,

and sending a copy of the letter written by the heart-broken mother.

Still war is war; and one of its laws is, that, if a prisoner is unjustly killed by an enemy, one of the enemy's men held as prisoner shall be killed in retaliation, the object being, of course, to put a stop to unjust executions. With this law in view, Congress did not consent to countermand the young man's execution.

Captain Asgill had another friend, a powerful one, who did all that he could to save him from his impending fate. This was General Washington, who from the first had pitied the young man on account of his youth and general character; but he had also objected to the selection for the reason that he had been among the officers who surrendered with Lord Cornwallis, who had been promised that they should not be dealt with as hostages. There were other prisoners who might have been more justly taken as subjects of retaliation, but for some reason the thirteen officers who had been summoned to this trial by lot were not among those who were justly liable in the case. Washington felt that the selection of Asgill was a breach of good faith, and he did all that he could to induce the secretary of war to act justly and honorably in the matter. At all events, the efforts in behalf of the young officer had the effect of delaying the execution; and three months after his fatal lot had been drawn, he was allowed to go to Morristown and remain there a prisoner on parole.

Not long after this, another reason arose for the

pardon of Captain Asgill, which was used with effect by his friends. Peace was now approaching, and there was no need of the execution of hostages in order to prevent further outrages on the part of the enemy; and so the members of Congress began to feel that after this long delay, and the approaching general rejoicing in the success of American independence, it would seem like murder to execute this young man. Therefore a law was passed by Congress, directing that Captain Asgill should be set at liberty and allowed to return to his family.

Dreadful months of suspense and fearful anticipation had darkened the souls of this young soldier, his family, and his friends; but they had probably produced a better effect upon the minds of the lawless bands of Tory refugees than would have resulted had the execution taken place; for, had Captain Asgill been hung, there is no doubt that an American prisoner would have suffered in his place; and how many more steps in the bloody business of retaliation would have taken place, no man can tell. So, if we look at the matter philosophically, it may have been a very good thing that the British officer selected to atone for the death of Captain Huddy happened to be a young man whom nobody wished to kill, for the merciful delay exercised in his case was the probable cause of the cessation of retaliation during the last months of the Revolution.

THE STORY OF TEMPE WICK.

THERE are so many curious and unexpected things which may happen in time of war, especially to people who live in parts of a country where the enemy may be expected to come, or where the friendly army is already encamped, that it is impossible to guard against unpleasant occurrences; and it often happens that the only thing to be depended upon when an emergency arises, is presence of mind, and quickness of wit.

In these qualities, New Jersey girls have never shown themselves behind their sisters of other parts of the country, and a very good proof of this is shown by an incident which took place near Morristown during the time that the American army was quartered in that neighborhood.

Not far from the town was a farm then known as Wick's farm, situated in a beautiful wooded country. The daughter of Mr. Wick, named Tempe (probably short for Temperance), was the owner of a very fine horse, and on this beautiful animal it was her delight to ride over the roads and through the woods of the surrounding country. She had been accustomed to horses since she was a child, and was not afraid to ride anywhere by herself.

When she first began to canter over these hills and dales, it had been in times of peace, when there was nothing in this quiet country of which any one might be afraid; and now, although these were days of war, she felt no fear. There were soldiers not far away, but these she looked upon as her friends and protectors; for Washington and his army had encamped in that region to defend the country against the approach of the enemy. If any straggling Redcoats should feel a desire to come along the hills, they would be very apt to restrain their inclinations so long as they knew that that brave American army was encamped near by.

So Miss Tempe Wick, fearing nothing, rode far and wide, as she had been in the habit of doing, and every day she and her good steed became better and better acquainted with each other.

One fine afternoon, as Tempe was slowly riding homeward, within a mile of her house, she met half a dozen soldiers in Continental uniform, and two of them, stepping in front of her, called upon her to stop. When she had done so, one of them seized her bridle. She did not know the men; but still, as they belonged to Washington's army, who were her countrymen and friends, she saw no reason to be afraid, and asked them what they wanted.

At first she received no answer, for they were very busily occupied in looking at her horse and expressing their satisfaction at the fine points of the animal. Tempe had had her horse praised before; but these men were looking at him, and talking about him, very much as if he were for sale and they were thinking of buying. Presently one of the men said to her that this was a very excellent horse that she was riding, and they wanted it. To this Tempe exclaimed, in great amazement, that it was her own horse, that she wanted him herself, and had no wish to dispose of him. Some of the soldiers laughed, and one of them told her that the troops were about to move, and that good horses were greatly needed, and that they had orders to levy upon the surrounding country and take horses wherever they could find them.

Now was Tempe astonished beyond measure. If half a dozen British soldiers had surrounded her, and had declared that they intended to rob her of her horse, she would not have wondered at it, for they would have taken it as the property of an enemy. But that the soldiers of her own country, the men on whom she and all her friends and neighbors depended for protection and safety, should turn on her and rob her, as if they had been a set of marauding Hessians, was something she could scarcely comprehend.

But it did not take her long to understand, that no matter who they were or what they were, — whether they thought they had a right to do what they threatened, or whether they had no regard for right and justice, — they were in earnest, and intended to take her horse. When this conviction flashed into the mind of Tempe Wick, there also flashed into it a determination to show these men that a Jersey girl had a will of her own, and that if they wanted her property, they would have to do a great deal more than simply to come to her and ask her to hand it over to them.

After a little parley, during which the man who held her bridle let go of it, supposing she was about to dismount, she suddenly gave her spirited horse a sharp cut with the whip, dashed between two of the soldiers, and, before they could comprehend what had happened, she was off and away.

As fast as they could run, the soldiers followed her, one or two of them firing their guns in the air, thinking to frighten her and make her stop; but, as though she had been a deer and her pursuers ordinary hunters, she swiftly sped away from them.

But they did not give up the chase. Some of them knew where this girl lived, and were confident that when they reached her house, they would have the horse. If they had known it was such a fine animal, they would have come after it before. According to their belief, good horses should go into the army, and people who staid at home, and expected other people to fight for them, ought to be willing to do what they could to help in the good cause, and at least give their horses to the army.

As Tempe sat upon her bounding steed, she knew very well that the soldiers could never catch her; but her heart sank within her as she thought of what would happen when they came to the farm and demanded her horse. Running away from them was only postponing her trouble for a little while, for there was no one about the place who could prevent those

men from going to the
barn and taking away
the animal.

It would be of no use
to pass her house and
ride on and on. Where
should she go? She must
come back some time, and
all the soldiers would
have to do would be to
halt at the farm, and wait
until she returned. And
even if she should take
her horse into the wood
and tie him to a tree, they would know by her coming back on foot that she had left him at no great
distance, and they would be sure to follow his tracks
and find him.

As Tempe rode swiftly on, her thoughts galloped
as fast as her horse, and before she reached the
house she had come to a conclusion as to the best
thing to be done. She did not ride towards the
barn, but dashed through the gateway of the large
yard, and sprang from her steed. As she turned in,
she looked down the road; but the men were not in
sight. What she was going to do was something
which people never did, but it was the only thing
she could think of, and she was a girl whose actions
were as quick as her ideas were original. Without
stopping an instant, she took her horse to the back
door, and led him boldly into the house.

This was not the sort of stable to which Tempe's horse or any other American horse was accustomed; but this animal knew his mistress, and where she led, he was willing to follow. If one of the farm hands had attempted to take the creature into the house, there would probably have been some rearing and plunging; but nothing of this kind happened as our Jersey girl, with her hand on her horse's bridle, led him quickly inside and closed the door behind him. As the story goes, she took him through the kitchen, and then into the parlor, without the slightest regard to the injury his shoes might do to the well-kept floor; and from the parlor she led him into a bedroom on the lower floor, which was usually used as a guest chamber, but which never before had such a guest as this.

This room had but a single window, the shutters of which were kept closed when it was not in use, and there was no entrance to it except through the door which opened from the parlor. The door was quickly closed, and Tempe stood with her horse in the darkness.

When the soldiers reached the farm, they went to the barn. They examined the outhouses, visited the pasture fields, and made a thorough search, high and low, near and far; but no sign of a horse could they find. Of course, the notion that the animal was concealed in the house did not enter their minds, and the only way in which they could account for the total disappearance of the horse was, that Tempe had ridden off with him — where they knew not. We do

not know how long they waited for the sight of a
hungry horse coming home to his supper, but we do
know that while there was the slightest danger of
her dear horse being taken away from her, that animal remained a carefully attended guest in the spare
room of the Wick house; and the tradition is, that

he staid there three weeks. There Tempe waited
on him as if he had been a visitor of high degree;
and if she was afraid to go to the barn to bring him
hay and oats, she doubtless gave him biscuit and
soft bread, — dainties of which a horse is very fond,
especially when they are brought to him by such a
kind mistress as Tempe.

When the cavalry moved away from their camp near Morristown, no one of them rode on that fine horse on which they had seen a girl gayly cantering, and which, when they had been about to put their hands upon it, had flown away, like a butterfly from under the straw hat of a schoolboy. When the troops were gone, the horse came out of the guest chamber and went back to his stall in the stable; and that room in which he passed so many quiet days, and the door through which the horse timidly stepped under the shadow of that hospitable roof, are still to be seen at the old Wick house, which stands now, as it stood then, with its shaded yard and the great willow tree behind it, on the pleasant country road by which we may drive from Morristown to Mendham by the way of Washington Corner.

THE STORY OF FORT NONSENSE.

DURING three years of the Revolution the American army, under General Washington, wintered in New Jersey. Of course, we understand, that, when an army goes into winter quarters, it does so because the weather prevents operations in the field; and although Washington did not in the least object to fighting in the cold weather if a good opportunity showed itself, as we know from the fact that he fought the battle of Trenton on Christmas Day, still the winters in New Jersey were for the most part periods of inactivity.

Histories give us full accounts of the important battles and marches which took place in New Jersey; but the life of the army in the long, cold months in which fighting and marching were almost impossible, is something with which we are not so well acquainted; and when we understand what the men of our army were obliged to suffer and to endure, and the responsibilities and anxieties which were so conscientiously borne by Washington and his officers, we are compelled to give as much credit to the soldiers of the Revolution for their heroism in their winter camps as for their courage upon the battlefield.

This winter life in New Jersey, of men and officers from New England, the Middle States, Virginia, and the Sóuth, appears to us now as very interesting, and in many ways a curious life. Into a quiet country neighborhood there came an entirely novel element, — an army which had not come there to fight, but to live.

Washington's first winter in New Jersey was spent in Morristown in 1777. This place was chosen because it was a productive country, and well situated for sudden expeditions against the enemy in that part of the State. Although there was no fighting done in Morristown, so many small detachments of 'troops went out from the place, and so many sudden attacks were made upon the outposts of the enemy in the country round about, that by the end of the winter the British had no hold in New Jersey except at Perth Amboy and New Brunswick.

But, as has been said before, it is not with the military operations that we are concerned, but with the winter life of the army in the camp. The first thing that has to be done when an army arrives to settle and make itself a home in and about a country town, is to provide a good house for the commander in chief and officers, and a suitable camping place for the men. Washington went to Arnold's Tavern, a large house on the corner of the Green; and the army encamped in the valley of the Loantika, a beautiful place in summer, but not particularly attractive in cold weather. Here they built themselves huts of logs, and here they tried to keep themselves warm and to be satisfied with what they had; for the government was poor, and found it hard to keep an army. There was plenty to eat and drink in the surrounding country, but there was very little money with which to buy it.

It was a great thing for the Morristown people to see the tavern surrounded night and day by a guard of twenty-six soldiers, and to have their streets and roads made lively by soldiers on foot, clad in the various uniforms worn by the men from different States, — some with cocked hats, some with round hats with feathers stuck in them; some with green coats, some with blue; some with buckskin breeches, others with black, — while Washington, with the officers of his staff, galloped here and there, dressed in the regular Continental uniforms of blue and buff.

Among the most conspicuous uniforms of the American army was that of the Jersey Blues. This was a volunteer organization formed in Essex County; and the first uniforms of these soldiers were furnished by the patriotic women of that region. They were not able to afford anything handsome or costly: so each soldier was provided with a frock coat and trousers made of tow cloth, which was dyed a bright blue by the same women who made it into soldiers' clothes. These Jersey Blues, although they must have presented a very peculiar appearance in the field, became famous soldiers, and were known throughout the war, and occupied high positions in the Continental army. The Jersey Blues were never disorganized, and still remain prominent among the citizen soldiers of the State.

It was Washington's habit during the war, as soon as he had settled himself in his winter quarters, to send for Mrs. Washington to join him; and accordingly she came to Morristown very soon after his first arrival there. Men and officers were always delighted when the wife of the commander in chief came down to live among them, and they welcomed the sight of the carriage drawn by four horses, with the postilions and grooms dressed in Washington's own livery of scarlet and white. On this occasion, Washington went some distance to meet his wife, and waited in a little village until she should arrive.

When the lady at the house where he was stopping
saw the grand carriage drive up, she was prepared to
behold an illustrious personage alight from it, and she
was somewhat surprised when she saw a very plainly
dressed, quiet lady step down from the high coach.
She thought there surely must be some mistake; but
when she saw the courteous affection with which the
grand gentleman in the fine uniform and cocked hat
greeted this plainly dressed lady, she knew that she
had made no mistake.

There was no ostentation or superciliousness about
Mrs. Washington. She was hospitable and kind, and
she put on no airs because she was a great lady from
Virginia, and because she was the wife of the commander in chief of the army. The story is told, that,
soon after her arrival, some ladies of the town went to
pay their respects to her, and as they were going
to visit the first lady of the land, they thought that
they should dress themselves in their finest clothes.
Arrayed in silks, satins, and ruffles, they were shown
into the presence of Mrs. Washington, and were utterly
amazed to find her wearing a striped homespun apron,
and busily engaged in knitting stockings. She received them, however, with as much dignity and
courtesy as if she had had a crown on her head and
a scepter in her hand; and in the course of conversation she said that it was the duty of every one to
try to do without the things which they were obliged
to buy from foreign countries, and to make for themselves, as far as possible, what they needed; and that,
while their husbands and brothers were fighting in the

field, she thought that they should do what they could at home to help the great cause.

Mrs. Washington entertained the ladies with accounts of her life at home. She said that in her house there were always sixteen spinning wheels at work. She showed them two morning dresses which had been made in her house from ravelings of old satin chair covers. But Mrs. Washington was not at all averse to cheerfulness and good company, and in that year there were many dances and parties in Morristown, which kept the place quite gay.

Two years afterwards, Washington and his army wintered at Middlebrook, in Somerset County. Here the army had a comparatively comfortable time, for the weather was mild, without much snow or frost; and this, after the terrible sufferings which they had had at Valley Forge the winter before, was very well calculated to put men as well as officers in a cheerful state of mind. It is true that the difficulties of obtaining provisions were in some ways greater than they had been before; for the Continental money, with which all supplies were paid for, was depreciating so rapidly that now thirty or forty dollars of it were barely equal to one silver dollar, and the country people very much disliked to take it. But the army had just achieved some important victories, and there was a feeling in many circles that it would not be long before the war would end; and with this belief in the minds of many, and with the general satisfaction in the mild and pleasant weather, it is no wonder that there were some good times in the army during that winter at Middlebrook.

General Washington always liked to have company at dinner, for he was very hospitable, and, besides this, he considered it his duty to become acquainted with his officers and with the people of the neighborhood; and sometimes as many as thirty persons sat down at the table. Even if the various articles of food were not of the finest quality, they were well cooked and well served. While in Middlebrook, Washington desired a dinner service of white queen's-ware, and he wrote to Philadelphia to obtain it. Among the articles he mentioned in his order were eight dozen shallow plates and three dozen soup plates, which gives an idea of the size of his dinner parties. But, although Philadelphia was searched from one end to the other, no queen's-ware of the kind could be found, and at last Washington was told that he could get what he wanted in New Brunswick, and there he bought his queen's-ware.

Among other things which he ordered at that time were "six tolerably genteel but not expensive candlesticks;" and he also wrote for a new hat, stating, "I do not wish by any means to be in the extreme of fashion, either in the size or manner of cocking it."

At these dinners there was a good deal of state and ceremony, although the heads of the family were very courteous and attentive to their guests. As this was a military establishment, everything was done promptly and according to rule. Washington never waited longer than five minutes for any guest who was late. When such a person did arrive after the company had seated themselves at the table, he would always try to put him at his ease by some pleasant remark, sometimes saying that he had a cook "who never asks whether the company has come, but whether the hour has come."

During this winter a great entertainment was given by General Knox and some other officers, and it was said to be the finest thing of the kind ever seen in that part of the State. It may be thought, and probably there were people who thought it then, that at a time when money was so much needed, and provisions were so hard to get, a great and expensive festival like this was extravagant and out of place; but it is likely that the gayety of that great day had a good and encouraging effect upon the army as well as the people of the country. They knew why the day had been celebrated, and because of the general rejoicings they believed there was reason to rejoice; and when people believe that there is a good thing coming, they are much more ready to fight for it than if they had no such belief.

But it is not of these two winters that our story has to deal: it is with the second encampment at Morristown, during the cold, the snow, and the icy

frosts of 1779–80. At this time, General and Mrs.
Washington lived in the handsome house which is now
known as "Washington's Headquarters," and has been
preserved in the same condition as it was in those
Revolutionary days. In this fine old mansion, General
Washington and his wife kept up their hospitable
customs; and at their table were seen such men as
Alexander Hamilton, General Greene, Baron Steuben,
Kosciusko, Pulaski, "Light Horse Harry" Lee, Israel
Putnam, "Mad Anthony" Wayne, and Benedict Arnold.
There also came to Morristown the minister from
France (the Chevalier de la Luzerne) and an envoy
from Spain (Don Juan de Mirailles). These two distinguished foreigners were received with great honor.
An escort was sent out to meet them; there was a
grand review of the troops, in which Washington and
his generals, together with the Frenchman and the
Spaniard, appeared on the field, splendidly mounted;
while on the grand reviewing stand was the governor
of the State and a great many citizens and distinguished people. After a salute of thirteen cannon, the
parading army went through its evolutions, and in the
evening there was a grand ball.

But one of the guests to whom these honors were
given did not appear at the ball. The Spanish envoy
was taken sick, and a few days afterwards died at
the headquarters. He was buried with great pomp
and ceremony. The funeral procession was a mile
long, and attended by Washington and all his officers.
Minute guns boomed as the procession passed from
the headquarters to the graveyard at the back of the

First Presbyterian Church, and people came from all parts of the surrounding country to view the great procession.

The funeral services were conducted by a Spanish priest with the impressive rites of the Catholic Church; and after a military salute had been fired over the grave, sentinels were placed to guard it, for the Spanish nobleman was buried in full regalia. A gold watch studded with diamonds was in his pocket; diamonds were on his fingers; and valuable seals were attached to his watchguard.

There was not so much fear at this time of an attack from the enemy as there had been during the previous winter, when Washington was at Morristown. Now, there were only four guards at the headquarters, — two at the front of the house, and two at the back. But the most careful preparations were made in case the enemy should show itself, and now and then a false alarm showed the perfection of the discipline which was maintained.

On such occasions a shot would be heard from one of the most distant outposts, then a sentinel near the town would fire, and so on until a report would be heard by the sentinels at the headquarters, who would fire their guns; then there were the guns in Morristown, and so on out to the camp, and very soon a detachment would hurry into the town at a quick-step. But before they reached the place, the life guard encamped near the headquarters would rush to the house, enter the lower story, and barricade the doors; and five men at each window, with muskets loaded and ready to fire, would await the approach of the enemy.

But although no British soldiers ever reached Morristown, there was good reason for all the pre-cautions taken. Besides the frequent attempts which were made by large bodies of the Redcoats to penetrate to the region occupied by Washington's army, there were small expeditions even more dangerous. One of these consisted of a party of picked British cavalry-men, who started from their camp near New York, by way of Elizabethtown, for the express purpose of capturing General Washington. They advanced in the direction of Morristown until they reached Chatham, about six miles distant, and there — being overtaken by a terrible storm, and finding so many difficulties ahead of them — they gave up their project.

Outside of Morristown, on a high hill which stretches away to the southwest, the American army was en-camped during this winter. Among these men we can scarcely believe there were many festivities or merrymakings. In fact, the sufferings and privations of the common soldiers at this time were very great, and even the table of the commander in chief was sometimes furnished with the plainest of food. In a letter written by Washington at this time, he says, —

"We have had the virtue and patience of the army put to the severest trial. Sometimes it has been five or six days together without bread; at other times as many days without meat; and once or twice, two or three days without either. I hardly thought it possible, at one period, that we should be able to keep it together, nor could it have been done, but for the exertions of the magistrates in the several counties of this state [Jersey], on whom I was obliged to call, expose our situation to them, and in plain terms declare that we were reduced to the alternative of disbanding or catering for ourselves, unless the inhabitants would afford us their aid. I allotted to each county a certain proportion of flour or grain, and a certain number of cattle, to be delivered on certain days; and for the honor of the magistrates, and the good disposition of the people, I must add that my requisitions were punctually complied with, and in many counties exceeded. Nothing but this great exertion could have saved the army from dissolution or starving, as we were bereft of every hope from the commissaries. At one time the soldiers ate every kind of horse food but hay. Buckwheat, common wheat, rye, and Indian corn composed the meal which made their bread. As an army, they bore it with the most heroic patience; but sufferings like these, accompanied by the want of clothes, blankets, etc., will produce frequent desertions in all armies; and so it happened with us, though it did not excite a single mutiny."

At this time, various circulars and printed bills were sent to the American army from the British, urging the men to fly from all their hardships and miseries, and join the English force, where they would be received, and furnished with every comfort. In this condition of things it was very important to keep the American soldiers, cold, hungry, and idle, from thinking too much of their troubles. Washington could not give them balls, nor invite them to dine; but he wisely considered that the best thing he could give them was occupation, — a most wonderful medicine for discontent. He therefore determined to build a fort upon the summit of the hill where the camp was situated.

His engineers therefore planned a large fortification made up of earthworks; and on this the men were put to work, as if it had been expected that the enemy would soon arrive, and take the place. The desire to put their camp in a condition of defense, and the animation of steady labor, were of as much advantage to the spirits of the soldiers as bread and meat would be to their bodies; and, from sitting in idle groups about their camp fires and huts, they worked on the new intrenchments, ramparts, and redoubts with cheerful energy.

Everything was done exactly as if the new fort were soon to be called upon to protect the town, which stretched itself beneath the hill; and the engineers and officers were as careful in making plans and giving directions as if they had been building a fort at the entrance of New York Bay.

It was never expected that the fort would be attacked, and it was never supposed, that, if the British should come this way, the battle would be fought in or about the town; but the building of the fort was honestly intended for the defense and protection of the troops, not against muskets, cannon, and bayonets, but against discontent and despair, — enemies far more formidable to the suffering army of that day than British troops and Hessians.

The result was a good one: Washington's army at Morristown stood by him as long as he staid there;

and when they marched away, they left upon the top of that hill a monument to the wisdom, the kindness, and the knowledge of human nature, displayed by their great commander in chief in those hazardous days.

We do not know what this earthwork was first called; but in time it came to be known as Fort Nonsense, simply because it appeared to the ordinary man as a great piece of work undertaken without any good purpose. But never was a name more inapplicable. If it had been called Fort Good Sense, it would have been much more suitable.

The remains of this fort are still to be seen on the hill beyond Morristown; and a monumental stone has been set up there to mark its site, and explain its nature and purpose. Most of its ramparts and redoubts have been washed away by the storms of more than a century, and we can still perceive many of its outlines; but those skilled in the art of military fortification know that it was a good fortress, while students of human nature and of the influence of great minds upon the welfare of their fellow-beings, know that it acted an important part in the defense of our liberties and the establishment of our government.

It may be remarked that in this story we have said a good deal about other things, and very little about Fort Nonsense. But there is very little of Fort Nonsense, and not much to say about it; and what has been told was the story of the camp life of Washington and his army in New Jersey, the most permanent and suggestive point of which is the earthwork called Fort Nonsense.

AN AMERICAN LORD.

AMONG the principal men of colonial days and of Revolutionary times, there were many whose social positions were much the same as the station of the ordinary European aristocrat. From their ancestors the colonists had inherited the disposition to recognize differences in rank; and men of wealth and high position in the colonial government were regarded to a certain extent as members of the nobility are regarded in England. Before the Declaration of Independence, it was not even assumed in this country that all men are born equal.

But, although there were native-born personages in the Colonies who might well be termed aristocrats, their titles were political or military; and an American lord was, as he would be now, something entirely out of the common.

But in those days there was an American lord; and a very good American he was, in spite of his being a lord. This was William Alexander, known as Lord Stirling. He was born in New York, of Scotch parents. When he was quite a young man, he went into military life, and served in the British colonial army in the French War. In the campaigns in which he served, he gained the military education which was afterwards of the greatest advantage, not only to him, but to the country.

There was no British heir to the earldom of Stirling, a Scotch peerage; and, as he believed that he was a direct descendant of the last Lord Stirling, the young man went to England, and laid claim to the estate and title. He was successful in proving his direct descent from the earls of Stirling; but the House of Lords, who gave the final decision in the case, would not allow his claim. Even if the law had permitted his claim, it is not likely that the British House of Lords would have been anxious to welcome into the peerage an American-born person.

But although he got nothing more, he really obtained his title, and he was known then, as he is known in history, as Lord Stirling. He was a man of wealth, and must have had a very good time in England, for he studied well the manners and customs of the nobility; and as his own habits and tastes were those which he observed in the great houses of England, he here received a social education which had a great effect upon his future career.

He was also the means of educating some of the inhabitants of Great Britain, and the way in which he did it is shown by a little incident which occurred when he was visiting Scotland. He was invited to dine at the house of a gentleman, who informed his wife that an American was coming to take dinner with them. It is to be presumed that this announcement had about the same effect upon her as would now be produced if an American gentleman should inform his family that a chief from Madagascar was to dine with them.

The Scotch lady, no doubt, expected to see a copper-colored brave, in war paint and feathers, with toma-hawk, and bows and arrows, and perhaps a few scalps hanging from his belt. Probably she had busied herself devising a dinner which would suit a savage who was a native of that far-away land of America, and hoped she might give him something which would compen-sate him for the loss of a cannibal repast; but when she beheld the handsome young gentleman who came into the house with her husband, she could not repress her astonishment, and exclaimed, " Bless my soul! The animal is white." Ignorance of foreign countries was at that time not uncommon in Great Britain.

Although born in New York, Lord Stirling estab-lished himself in New Jersey, and it was in connec-tion with this State that he was afterwards generally known. His father had owned a large tract of land at Basking Ridge, a beautifully situated town not far from Morristown; and here Lord Stirling built him-self a stately mansion with fine gardens, and a great park in which were herds of deer. It was built in the fashion of the lordly country seats of England, around a courtyard paved with flagstones, and con-tained grand halls and stately apartments beautifully ornamented and furnished. The barns and outbuild-ings were grand, like the mansion itself, with cupolas and gilded vanes, and altogether the establishment was imposing and beautiful.

This young man had brought
with him from England servants,
butlers, valets, hairdressers, and
a great many fine horses, and
carriages with arms emblazoned
upon their panels. He
lived in grand state, and his
house was generally filled with
guests; for the best people of
the country were glad to visit
this beautiful home, where the
best of company and the freest
hospitality were always to be
found. The lord of the
manor was an affable
and courteous gentle-
man, and the writers of
those days have given
glowing accounts of the
gracious Lady Stirling and
her charming daughter, Lady Kitty.

But notwithstanding the fact that he felt as a lord
and lived as a lord, this grand gentleman never forgot

that he was not only a lord, but an American; and when the Colonies began to assert their claim to independence, Lord Stirling promptly showed his colors on the patriotic side. He commanded the first body of troops raised in New Jersey in the colonial days, and he very soon became one of the most prominent officers in the Revolutionary army.

After he was made general, he distinguished himself at the battle of Long Island, where he performed some daring feats. The odds were greatly against the Americans on that occasion, and, in order to secure the retreat of the main part of his command, Lord Stirling took four hundred men, and made a bold attack upon a house that was occupied by the British general, Cornwallis. During the desperate fight which followed, in which his little force was far outnumbered by the enemy, his command made a successful retreat, but he himself was captured, and afterwards imprisoned on a war ship.

But he did not stay there long. Washington could not do without the services of this man, who was not only a most earnest patriot, but an educated and efficient soldier; and, as the Americans held several English officers as prisoners of war, one of them was exchanged, with the least possible delay, for Lord Stirling.

One of the earliest and most daring exploits of this brave soldier was the capture, by an infantry force, of an armed British ship which was on its way to Boston with stores and supplies for the English army there.

This vessel, which was called the "Blue Mountain Valley," had met with rough weather, and, having been badly damaged, was lying off Sandy Hook, waiting for assistance from two British men-of-war then in New York Harbor.

But Lord Stirling, who was stationed not far from the coast, and to whom the situation of the vessel became known, determined that, if possible, he would get to this valuable storeship before the enemy's men-of-war could reach her. So, with a number of the regular soldiers under his command, and some volunteers from the neighborhood, he put out to sea in some small craft, one of them a pilot boat. The English vessel had for her defense six guns, and was what is called an armed transport, but Stirling's men carried only ordinary muskets. However, they boldly attacked the vessel, and bearing down upon her as if she had been a column of infantry, in spite of the cannon and guns of the crew, captured her.

As soon as this victory had been won, Lord Stirling had all sails set; and the "Blue Mountain Valley" waited no longer for the men-of-war to come to her assistance, but sailed away for Perth Amboy, which was in possession of the Americans. Here she was found to be a most valuable prize, although Lord Stirling was sorry, as he afterwards stated when he made his report to Congress, that her cargo was not arms, instead of coal and provisions.

Lord Stirling fought well in the battles of New Jersey. At Monmouth he especially distinguished himself by the way in which he managed the artillery which was under his command; and it is said that the enemy were amazed to find batteries so splendidly handled in the ranks of the Americans, who were not supposed by most British officers to be possessed of great military ability, although the erroneousness of this supposition was gradually impressed upon their minds as the war went on.

Our nobleman, however, had given another proof of his ability to adapt himself to military circumstances. When Washington and his army were wintered at Morristown, there was an evident desire among the British commanders to attack him at that place, and there was constant danger of an advance from the forces about New York. Lord Stirling was with the troops under General Greene, defending the principal approaches to Morristown on the east, and he very often had fights and skirmishes with British detachments sent out to reconnoiter the country, or to break into the American lines.

At one time a very large force, led by Clinton, advanced towards Morristown; and this was believed to be a serious and determined attempt to attack Washington, whose army was in a pretty bad plight, and not at all prepared to fight large bodies of well-appointed troops. Lord Stirling, with the other officers of the regular army, aided by forces of militiamen greatly excited by atrocities which had been committed by the British troops in the neighborhood, made a determined stand in the region of the "Short Hills," and a battle was fought near Springfield. Although the American forces were not able to defeat the

British, they so harassed them, placing themselves in all the passes through which it was necessary to advance, that at last the Redcoats gave up the attempt to reach Morristown, and retired to Elizabeth.

Throughout the war, this gentleman with the grand house, the park, the deer, the splendid carriages, the butlers, and the hairdressers, fought as earnestly and as patriotically as if he had been a sturdy farmer who had left his cornfield for the battlefield, with an old blunderbuss over his shoulder. Not only was he a good soldier, but he was a trustworthy friend to the cause of the Colonies and to General Washington; and it is said that it was through his means that the conspiracy among some of the officers of the army against General Washington, of whom they were jealous, was discovered and broken up.

Officers of the army were frequently quartered at his house at Basking Ridge, where they found most delightful company; and in every way our American lord did what he could for the cause and the people who were defending it. His title was generally recognized; and Washington, who was very particular in regard to matters of rank and social propriety, always called him "my lord." He was said to be a fine-looking man; in fact, he and Washington were of more imposing and dignified appearance than any other officers of the American army.

Of course, as he was a very notable person among the Continental officers, the British were very anxious to capture him. In 1781, when he was in command of the Northern Department at Albany, this design of the enemy came very near being carried out, but was frustrated by the faithful services of one of those good women who were continually turning up in colonial history. A servant girl in the family of a house near Albany, where Lord Stirling was staying, had been visiting her parents during the day, and had there heard a plot of the Tories of the neighborhood to capture Lord Stirling. Being of a patriotic disposition, she told her mistress of the plot as soon as she got home; and when in the night a large body of the enemy came to the house, they were met with a surprise.

Lord Stirling had not gone out of town without taking with him a guard of dragoons; and these men, instead of being quartered at a distance, as the Tories evidently supposed they would be, had all been brought into the house; and when the attack was made in the night, the bullets and pistol balls which whizzed and whistled from that ordinarily peaceful mansion astonished the Tories, who fled.

But although Lord Stirling did so much for American independence, he did not live to enjoy the fruits of it, for he died in Albany, while still in command of the Northern Department. After his death, the estate at Basking Ridge was sold, and payment for it was made in Continental money, which afterwards became of almost no value; so that for this fine property, it might be said, his family received nothing but a pile of badly printed paper. The mansion and the deer park and the emblazoned carriages are gone and forgotten; but the brave soldier, who gave up all the pleasures of a lordly position for his country, will live in history.

MOLLY PITCHER.

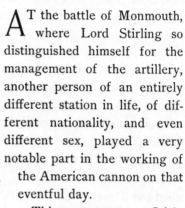

AT the battle of Monmouth, where Lord Stirling so distinguished himself for the management of the artillery, another person of an entirely different station in life, of different nationality, and even different sex, played a very notable part in the working of the American cannon on that eventful day.

This was a young Irishwoman, wife of an artilleryman. She was of a different disposition from ordinary women, who are glad enough to hide themselves in places of safety, if there is any fighting going on in their neighborhood. Molly was born with the soul of a soldier, and, although she did not belong to the army, she much preferred going to war to staying at home and attending to domestic affairs. She was in the habit of following her husband on his various marches, and on the day of the Monmouth battle she was with him on the field.

The day was very hot. The rays of the sun came down with such force that many of the soldiers were taken sick and some died; and the constant discharges of musketry and artillery did not make the air any cooler. Molly devoted herself to keeping her husband as comfortable as possible, and she made frequent trips to a spring not far away to bring him water; and on this account he was one of the freshest and coolest artillerymen on the ground. In fact, there was no man belonging to the battery who was able to manage one of these great guns better than Pitcher.

Returning from one of her trips to the spring, Molly had almost reached the place where her husband was stationed, when a bullet from the enemy struck the poor man and stretched him dead, so that Molly had no sooner caught sight of her husband than she saw him fall. She ran to the gun, but scarcely had reached it before she heard one of the officers order the cannon to be wheeled back out of the way, saying that there was no one there who could serve it as it had been served.

Now Molly's eyes flashed fire. One might have thought that she would have been prostrated with grief at the loss of her husband, but, as we have said, she had within her the soul of a soldier. She had seen her husband, who was the same to her as a comrade, fall, and she was filled with an intense desire to avenge his death. She cried out to the officer not to send the gun away, but to let her serve it; and, scarcely waiting to hear what he would say, she sprang to the cannon, and began to load it and fire it. She had so often attended her husband, and even helped him in his work, that she knew all about this sort of thing, and her gun was managed well and rapidly.

It might be supposed that it would be a very strange thing to see a woman on the battlefield firing a cannon; but even if the enemy had watched Molly with a spy-glass, they would not have noticed anything to excite their surprise. She wore an ordinary skirt, like other women of the time; but over this was an artillery-man's coat, and on her head was a cocked hat with some jaunty feathers stuck in it, so that she looked almost as much like a man as the rest of the soldiers of the battery.

During the rest of the battle, Molly bravely served her gun; and if she did as much execution in the ranks of the Redcoats as she wanted to do, the loss in the regiments in front of her must have been very great. Of course, all the men in the battery knew Molly Pitcher, and they watched her with the greatest interest and admiration. She would not allow any one to take her place, but kept on loading and firing until the work of the day was done. Then the officers and men crowded about her with congratulations and praise.

The next day General Greene went to Molly, — whom he found in very much the condition in which she had left the battlefield, stained with dirt and pow-der, with her fine feathers gone and her cocked hat dilapidated, — and conducted her, just as she was, to

General Washington. When the commander in chief heard what she had done, he gave her warm words of praise. He determined to bestow upon her a substantial reward; for any one who was brave enough and able enough to step in and fill an important place, as Molly had filled her husband's place, certainly deserved a reward. It was not according to the rules of war to give a commission to a woman; but, as Molly had acted the part of a man, Washington considered it right to pay her for her services as if she had been a man. He therefore gave her the commission of a sergeant, and recommended that her name be placed on the list of half-pay officers for life.

Every one in the army soon came to hear of the exploit of Molly Pitcher, and it was not long before she was called Captain Molly. The officers of the French regiment on the American side were particularly pleased with this act of heroism in a woman, and invited Molly to review their troops; and as she walked down the long line of soldiers, nearly every man put a piece of money in the cocked hat which she held in her hand.

This was the last battlefield on which Molly Pitcher appeared, but it had not been her first. Not long before, she had been with her husband in Fort Clinton when it was attacked by a very large force of the British. After a vigorous defense, the Americans found that it was impossible to defend the fort, and a retreat was ordered. As the soldiers were rushing out of the rear of the fort, Molly's husband turned away from his gun, threw down his match, — a piece of rope soaked in combustible substances, and slowly burning at one end, which was used in those days for discharging cannon, — and ran for his life. Molly prepared to follow him; but as she saw the glowing match on the ground, and knew that her husband's gun was loaded, she could not resist the desire to take one more crack at the enemy. So she stopped for an

instant,
picked up
the match,
touched off the
gun, and dashed
away after her husband.

The cannon which then blazed out in the face of the advancing British was the last gun which the Americans fired in Fort Clinton.

Molly did not meet with the reward which was accorded so many other Jersey women who were of benefit to their State and country. She died not long after the close of the war; and if she had known that she was to be famous as one of the heroes of the Revolution, there is no doubt that she would have hoped that people would be careful to remember that it was a man's service that she did to the country, and not a woman's.

But Captain Molly was not the only Jersey woman who was willing to act a man's part in the War for Independence. Among those of whom there is historical mention was Mrs. Jinnie Waglum, who lived near Trenton. At the time when Washington was arranging to march upon Princeton, she was visiting her friend, whose husband was the landlord of The True American Inn, just out of Trenton; and this tavern was Washington's headquarters at the time. In this way Mrs. Jinnie heard of the intended advance; and she also heard that there was no one in the American forces who knew the country well enough to conduct the army from Trenton to Princeton by any route except the highways, on which the advance would be observed by the enemy.

She therefore sent word to Washington that she would guide the army if he wished, and that there was no one who knew the country better than she did. Washington was a man who had sense enough to avail himself of good service whenever it was offered; and when he had made inquiries about Mrs. Waglum, he was perfectly willing to put his army under her guidance, and very glad indeed that she had offered her services.

When a woman acts the part of a man, it is not

surprising that she likes to look like a man; so Mrs. Jinnie put on a soldier's coat and a soldier's hat, and, mounting a horse, she headed the Continental army, commanded by Washington. This was a proud position, but she was equal to it; and on she rode, with all the cavalry and the infantry and the artillery and the general and staff following behind her. She took them along by Sand Town and Quaker Bridge, by roads over which she had often traveled; and the American army reached Princeton in good time for the battle which took place next day.

THE MORRISTOWN GHOSTS.

IN the early days of American history there was in New Jersey, as well as in New England and other parts of the country, a firm belief in the existence of witches and ghosts. Of course, there were people who knew enough not to put faith in supernatural apparitions and magical power; but there were so many who did believe in these things, that it was often unsafe, or at least unpleasant, to be an ugly old woman, or a young woman in not very good health, for it was believed that into such bodies the evil spirits delighted to enter.

Nearly all the older towns had their ghost stories, their witch stories, and their traditions of hidden treasure, guarded by spirits of persons who had been murdered, and buried with the gold in order that their spirits might act as a charm to frighten away anybody who should presume to dig in those spots. In Burlington were two great trees which were regarded with admiration and fear by many of the inhabitants. One was a large willow tree, which was called the Witches' Tree, around which these horrible spirits were supposed to dance on many a wild night. Another was the Pirates' Tree, a great walnut, under the roots of which many of the inhabitants firmly believed that the famous Blackbeard and his band had buried many pots of gold, silver, and precious stones; and these pots would have been dug up had it not been for the fear that the spirit of the savage pirate, who had been buried with the treasure, would have been the first thing to meet the eyes of the sacrilegious disturber of the pirate treasure vault.

There are other ghost stories of other places in New Jersey; but Morristown, some years after the close of the Revolution, took the lead of all the other Jersey towns as a scene of ghostly performances.

For years back many of the people had been convinced that an occasional witch had appeared among them, getting into the churns and preventing the butter from coming, breaking the legs of sheep in jumping over the fence, causing their horses to become suddenly mysteriously sick, and making themselves obnoxious in various ways. But it was not until the year 1788 that New Jersey ghosts determined to go regularly into business at this place.

Supernatural occurrences of this period attracted a great deal of attention, not only in the town itself, but in the surrounding country; and an account of what happened in Morristown during the time that the spirits were holding their visitations at that place is related in an old pamphlet published in 1792, written by an anonymous person who had no faith whatever in ghosts, but who had a firm belief in the efficacy of long words and complicated phraseology. We will take the story from this old pamphlet.

For a long time there had been a tradition that a vast treasure was buried on Schooley's Mountain, or, as it was then spelled, Schooler's Mountain, which was at that time a wild and desolate region more than twenty miles from Morristown. It is said that there were two gentlemen of the place who were particularly strong in their belief in this treasure, and they felt sure that all that was necessary in order to obtain it was to find some man who had knowledge of the habits and customs and requirements of the spirits in regard to treasures. Having their minds on this subject, it was not long before they heard of such a man. This was Mr. Ransford Rogers, a schoolmaster in Connecticut, who knew many things, and who pretended to know many more. He really did understand something about chemistry, was very ingenious and plausible, and had been frequently heard to say that he was not afraid of spirits, and was able to call them up, converse with them, and afterwards cause them to disappear. This was exactly the man needed by the two gentlemen of Morristown, and they went to Connecticut to see him.

When the business of the visitors was made known to Rogers, he was delighted, for here was an opportunity to get into a good business, which would probably be infinitely more pleasant than teaching. So he gave up his school and came to Morristown, being under contract to the two gentlemen to do what he could to induce the spirits to reveal the place of the concealed treasure in Schooley's Mountain. But as it would not do for a stranger to come into the town and hang out a sign, stating that he was a spirit raiser, it was necessary for Rogers to pretend that he had come on other business, and so he took charge of a small school outside of the town, but gave the greater part of his time to investigating the minds of the people of Morristown, in order that he might find out what he could do in the way of duping them; and in the words of the old writer, he found that this would be a good place for the "marvelous exhibitions which he was able to facilitate with the greatest alacrity."

Of course, he was not at all willing to begin business with the support of only two persons, and the first thing he did was to gather together as many men as possible who really wished to be rich, and who were willing to be governed by him in regard to the way in which they should go about obtaining the vast hoard buried far away in the mountain. After a time he succeeded in getting together as many as forty men, who all thoroughly believed in his honesty and in his ability to take them out to Schooley's Mountain, to call up the spirits who guarded the treasure, to induce them to turn it over to them, and then to vanish peaceably, without offering to molest or harm any one.

But it was a long time before Rogers was ready to lead his company on the great quest. There were many, many things that had to be done before they could start, and he soon found that he was not able to work out his great scheme alone; so he went back to Connecticut and got another schoolmaster, to whom he divulged his secret, and brought him to Morristown, and the two together went into the spirit business with great energy and enterprise. Night after night the company of treasure seekers met together, sometimes in a dark room, and sometimes out in the wild, lonely fields, close to black forests, and out of sight and hearing of human abodes.

Rogers was a chemist; and he frequently went out to one of these lonely meeting places in the afternoon and prepared a mine, which he exploded during the midnight meetings, and thus created a great wonder and terror among his followers. When they were indoors, there would be knockings and strange voices heard coming through the cracks; these voices proceeding from the other schoolmaster, who covered his mouth with what the writer of the pamphlet calls "a superficial machine," probably a bit of tin with a hole in it, which so disguised his voice that it was not recognized.

When they were out of doors in the black night, they would sometimes see a ghost flit about under the trees at the edge of the woods; and the second schoolmaster, well wrapped up in a sheet, seems to have made as good a ghost as could have been found anywhere. There were many supernatural performances, and among them was a great act, in which each one of the members of the company lay flat on his face in the field with his eyes shut, holding in one outstretched hand a sheet of paper. This was done in the hope that the spirits would write their instructions on the paper. Mr. Rogers knelt down with the others and held his paper; but it was not a blank sheet like the others. When this performance was over, all the papers were shaken together, and then they were drawn out one by one; and judge of the surprise and awe of all present, when one of them would contain some writing, — generally in a beautiful hand, such as could only be expected from a supernatural being (or a schoolmaster), — which would be found to be instructions as to what must be done.

The most important of these directions ordered that before any march could be made toward Schooley's Mountain, or any definite directions given in regard to the whereabouts of the treasure, each member should pay to the spirits, through Mr. Rogers, who would kindly act as agent, the sum of twelve pounds. And, moreover, this must not be paid in the paper money then current in New Jersey, which was called "loan money," and which would not pass outside of the State, but in gold or silver. When every member had paid in his twelve pounds, then the party would be led to the place of the treasure.

When they found out what they had to do, each man went to work to try, if possible, to raise the twelve pounds; but Rogers soon saw that it would be impossible for some of them to do this, as specie money was so hard to get, and he reduced the sum, in some cases, to six or four pounds. He was a good business manager, and would not try to get out of a man more than that man could pay.

Not one of the people engaged in this affair had the slightest idea that Rogers was deceiving them. It is not likely that any of them were people of much culture or means; and it is said that some of them went so far as to sell their cattle, and mortgage their farms, in order to get gold or silver to pay to the good schoolmaster who was generously acting as a mutual friend to both parties. But what were these sacrifices compared to the treasure they would obtain when at last they should be permitted to dig up the buried hoard on Schooley's Mountain!

It was now winter, and of course they could not start on the expedition in bad weather; but meeting after meeting was held, and it was at last definitely promised that the expedition should go forth from Morristown early in May. On the first of that month, they all gathered at midnight in the lonely field, and there was a terrible scene. There were more fire-works and explosions than usual, and one of the spirits appeared at the edge of the wood greatly excited, stamping his feet, and rushing about under the trees; and when Rogers went to see what was the matter,—for of course none of the others would dare to speak to a spirit,—he found that the supernatural beings with whom they had so long been in communication, and who were now scattered about in all parts of the woods, were very angry and incensed because they had become aware that some of the party were unfaithful, and had divulged the secrets which had been made known to them. They were so thoroughly indignant, in fact, that they refused to go on with the affair for a time, and announced that the expedition to Schooley's Mountain would be postponed until they were positively certain that every man who was to go there was the sort of man who would never let anybody into the awful, soul-dazzling secret which would be divulged. So they must all go home, and wait until this important matter could be satisfactorily arranged.

Strange to say, they all did go home, and waited, and not one of them suspected Rogers.

The schoolmaster had obtained a good deal of money, but he had not enough. So, in less than a month, he started another company, this time a small one, and began to go through his performances with them. But he soon found he could not make much money out of five men, and he began to get a little braver, and thought he would try what he could do with the better class of people in Morristown; and, having discovered that a very good ghost could be called up by means of a white sheet and a "superficial machine," he dressed himself up one night, and made a supernatural call upon a gentleman in good standing in the church. When he had appeared at the bedside of this good man, he told him all about the treasure of Schooley's Mountain, and, if he wanted some of it, how he might obtain it.

The gentleman, having never seen a ghost, supposed, of course, that this was an authorized apparition, and became greatly interested in what was told him. The next day, according to directions, he went around among his friends in the church, and soon formed a considerable company, who all believed, that, if they did what they were told to do, they could go to Schooley's Mountain and become immensely wealthy.

They did a great many things that they were told to do: they met in dark rooms, as the other party had met; they went out into a lonely field at midnight; they held out papers to be written on; and, more than that, they conducted their meetings with prayer and other solemnities. And they all promised to pay twelve pounds in gold as an earnest of their good faith in the spirits, and to deliver the money to that great miracle worker, Mr. Rogers, who would remit it to the spirits.

The schoolmaster found it necessary to be more mystical and weird in his dealings with this second party than with the first. He did a great many strange things which savored of magic and alchemy. Among other things, he got some fine bone dust, which he assured his followers was the dust of the bodies of the spirits who were to lead them to the treasure; and a little of this, wrapped up in a paper, he gave to each one of them, which they were to keep secret, and preserve as a magical charm.

One of the company, an old gentleman who was sometimes a little absent-minded, went to bed one night and left the magical packet in one of his pockets; and his wife, probably looking for small change, found it. She could not imagine what it was, but she was afraid it was something connected with witchcraft, and was greatly troubled about it. The next day she told her husband of the discovery, and was so very persistent that he should explain to her what it meant, that at last he thought it wise to tell her the whole proceeding, and so prevent her from interfering with the great and important business with which he was concerned. He made her promise secrecy, and soon she had heard all about Rogers, the spirits, and the buried gold. She became convinced that it was all the work of the devil, and she went off among her friends and began to talk about it.

Now there was a great excitement, not only on the part of the believers, but among the spirits themselves; and Rogers, who had enlisted two new men in his scheme, made his ghosts work hard to keep up the delusion among his followers. All four of them, dressed in sheets, went about making communications whenever they had a chance, and assuring the members of the band of treasure hunters that everything would soon be all right, and that they must not allow their faith to be shaken by gossipers and scandalmongers.

Rogers himself, in his ghostly costume, went one

night to the house of a gentleman who was his follower, and made some important communications to him; but as the schoolmaster had been encouraging himself by some strong drink before setting out on his round of apparitions, he talked in such a queer way to his disciple, that the latter became suspicious. The next morning he found horse tracks from his door to Rogers's house, and so discovered that the ghost had come from that place on horseback. Further investigations followed, and it was not long before it became quite plain that Rogers had been playing a well-planned trick upon the inhabitants of Morristown, and he was arrested.

Every one, however, had not lost faith in him, and there was an old gentleman — whose name the ancient pamphlet very kindly conceals, calling him by the name of "Compassion" — who went bail for him, and he was released; whereupon he and his friends decamped. However, Rogers was again arrested, and this time he confessed the whole of his share in raising the ghosts of Morristown.

But, as has been said, he was a man of ability, and able to take care of himself, and in some way he managed to escape from custody, and was seen no more in New Jersey. His followers, who had sent their gold and silver to the spirits by means of his kind offices, never saw their money again; and the vast treasures buried at Schooley's Mountain still remain hidden from all men.

A JERSEYMAN AND HIS ROYAL CROWN.

WE have told the story of the lord who lived at Basking Ridge; now we will tell the story of a much more exalted personage, one who had sat upon a throne, and worn a crown and royal robes rich with diamonds and precious stones, and who lived on a breezy hill on the banks of the Delaware. What he was doing in New Jersey, and how he had come to wear a crown and royal robes, we will now proceed to tell.

This exalted personage was not a king when he was living in New Jersey, but he had been a king. In fact, if we may not say that he had been two kings, we can say that he had been a king twice. He was Joseph Bonaparte, the eldest brother of the great emperor, Napoleon, who, after having conquered a great many nations of Europe, and having deposed their kings, supplied them with new sovereigns out of his own family. Joseph was sent to Italy to be King of Naples. He did not particularly want to be king, and he knew that the people did not want him, and after he had been in Naples some time, reigning under his brother's orders with no great success, the emperor determined to transfer him to Spain, whose throne had just been made vacant. Having been informed that he was to go to Madrid, Joseph obeyed, but he did not like it.

Moreover, the people of Spain did not like it, and after a time they rose up in rebellion, and were assisted by the English and Portuguese, and forced the king to fly from Spain.

The ex-king of Naples and Spain had various adventures in France and Switzerland; and when the power of the great Napoleon came to an end, he was obliged to fly, or he also might have been sent to Elba or some other place equally undesirable, so he determined to come to America. In a little brig of two hundred tons, a very small vessel to sail on the ocean, he crossed the Atlantic in disguise, not even the captain of the vessel knowing who he was. He was accompanied by his secretary; and when the two reached America and made themselves known, they were treated with great respect and attention. In fact, America owed so much to France, that she was very willing to show her gratitude.

Now that he was well out of Europe, Joseph Bonaparte gave up all idea of returning, and in deciding to settle here it was not surprising that he chose to make his home in New Jersey. He bought a place near Bordentown, on a high wooded hill called Point Breeze, and built a house, which was truly splendid for those days. It had grand halls and staircases and banquet halls, and it must have been larger and more imposing than Lord Stirling's. His estate, which covered more than a thousand acres, was beautifully laid out in drives and gardens and lawns, and everything on the place was arranged in a style of beauty and grandeur.

It was three years before this great house, with its surroundings, was finished, and ready for the ex-king's residence; and when at last he went there, he lived in ex-regal style. His wife was not with him, having remained in Italy on account of ill health, and her physicians would never allow her to come to America. But he had two daughters who were with him during part of his residence in New Jersey, and there were persons who asserted that he had also brought with him the crown of Spain and the royal robes of Italy.

It generally happens, when a sovereign is obliged to abdicate and to fly from his kingdom, that he arranges matters so that he shall not become a pauper when he arrives at the place of refuge. If he is not able to carry away anything more than a valise, he is much more likely to put his royal jewels into it than to fill it up with night clothes and hairbrushes; so when Bonaparte came to New Jersey, he came as a very rich man.

When his kingly mansion was ready to be supplied with art treasures, such as ornamented the palaces of Europe, the ex-king sent across the ocean for costly paintings and beautiful sculpture with which, to fill his new house; and if any crowned heads had happened to visit him, he would not have been ashamed to welcome them beneath his roof. People of royal blood — that is, the same kind of royal blood that he had — did come over to visit him. Louis Napoleon, afterward Emperor of France, came, when a young man, and spent some weeks with his uncle. While there, it is said, this young man went out shooting on the estate, and, finding the birds near the house easier to hit than those at a distance, he blazed away at any feathered creatures he saw in the garden, so that the gardener made a complaint.

But even then this young Louis Napoleon had begun to have dreams in regard to his succession to the imperial throne of France, and he did not like to be snubbed and scolded by an uncle who had had all the regal honors he was ever likely to get, and who therefore had no right to put on airs in his dealings with the prospective wearer of a crown. So there was a quarrel between the two, and there are reports to the effect that Louis Napoleon took revenge upon his uncle by cutting his fruit trees with a hatchet, without, however, imitating Washington in regard to subsequent truthfulness.

Besides visitors from abroad, many distinguished Americans visited the ex-king. Among these were Henry Clay, Daniel Webster, and John Quincy Adams.

General Lafayette, also, when he came to this country, was received with great state by the Count de Survilliers, the title under which Joseph Bonaparte lived at Bordentown.

This ex-king never became an American citizen by taking out naturalization papers; but the Legislature of New Jersey treated him very well, and passed a resolution which enabled him to hold property in this State, and to thus become, in fact, a Jerseyman.

But although our ex-king was now established on the free soil of America, he did not feel altogether safe. His family had come to grief; and there was reason to fear, that, as a member of that family, England, or France, or Spain, might demand him as a prisoner, to be taken across the ocean to answer the charge of unlawful occupation of a throne.

It is quite possible that the people of the neighborhood imagined that the ex-king was in greater fear of molestation from his former ròyal brethren than was really the case. Their reasons for supposing that he was anxious to defend himself against surprise and capture had some ground, for there were some strange things about that ex-royal estate, — things that were not known in any other part of New Jersey. There was a tall building called a belvedere, from which the country and the river might be surveyed for a long distance in every direction; but, stranger far than that, there were subterranean passages which led from the house to unfrequented parts of the grounds. These passages were well built, arched with brick, and high enough for people to walk upright in them; and

although persons of quiet and unimaginative minds
thought that they were constructed for the purpose
of allowing the occupants to go down to the lake or
to the other portions of the grounds without getting
wet if it should happen to be raining, there were many
people who believed that for sudden showers a good

stock of umbrellas would be cheaper and quite as
useful, and that these costly passages could be meant
for nothing else than to give opportunity for escape,
in case foreign emissaries or officers of the law should
come in search of an ex-king who was wanted on
the other side of the Atlantic.

For whatever reason these passages were built,
the spectacle of an ex-king, carrying a crown and his

royal robes in a hand bag, slipping out from among some bushes to tramp along the dusty road to Trenton or Burlington, was never seen. Nobody ever thought it worth while to come to New Jersey to demand him or his property.

During his residence at Bordentown, which continued for about fourteen years, Joseph Bonaparte was very popular with the people of the neighborhood. They looked upon him as a friend and neighbor; but at the same time they did not lose sight of the fact, that although he was now a country gentleman of New Jersey, with his lawn and his flower garden to look after, he had sat upon two thrones, and had been a sovereign of Naples and Spain. They called him "king," and his house was known as the "palace;" and for this reason the people of other States made some mild fun of New Jersey, calling it a foreign country.

But if this ex-king had been a rich country gentleman of the neighborhood, he could not have made himself more popular. He was hospitable, and frequently gave entertainments, and he sent flowers and fruits from his gardens to his friends and neighbors. He made roads, and contributed in many ways to the improvement of the country round about his home. In winter time the boys of Bordentown came to skate upon his ponds; and at such times he nearly always offered them refreshments, which consisted of quantities of chestnuts, which he scattered on the ice so that the youngsters might scramble for them.

In many ways his kind and sociable disposition made him so much liked, that it is very probable that if the officers of the law had come to take him back to Europe, he would have received such timely notice of their approach that it would not have been necessary for him to hurry away through his underground passages. New Jersey is a reasonable and hospitable State, and when an ex-king comes to reside within her borders, he will be as well treated, so long as he behaves himself, as if he were a poor immigrant from Europe, coming with his wife and family to clear away the forest, and make himself a home.

Just before Joseph started for America, the affairs of his family were at their lowest ebb. His great brother, the emperor, had fallen from his high state, and could look forward to nothing but imprisonment by the European countries, whose thrones he had for so long been in the habit of upsetting or threatening. In his last interview with Napoleon, when on his way to the ship which was to take him to America, Joseph generously offered to change places with his brother, and to let the ex-emperor fly to America instead of the ex-king. It was very difficult for any one of the Napoleon family to get away from France at that time; but Joseph had made a very excellent plan by which passports were provided for two persons coming to America on business, and his brother could have used one of those as well as himself.

But the great Napoleon declined to run away in this manner. He remained, and was sent to St. Helena. What would have occurred in the neighborhood of Bordentown, N.J., had Napoleon Bonaparte, conqueror of Europe, ruler of nations, and disposer of crowns, the hero of Austerlitz, Marengo, and Wagram, taken up his residence at Point Breeze, and established himself as a citizen of the State, cannot easily be imagined. The geniality, sociability, and hospitality of the ex-king could hardly have been expected from the ex-emperor; and, surrounded as he would have been in time by devoted followers who would have exiled themselves from their country for his sake, there might have been a little empire in New Jersey which would have been exceedingly interesting to tourists.

Moreover, if the allied powers of Europe had sent over a fleet to bring back their great enemy, who knows but that they might have found, when they reached Bordentown, not a tall lookout tower and underground passages for escape, but a fort with ramparts, redoubts, a moat, a drawbridge, and mounted cannon ready to sweep the Delaware and the surrounding country? However this might have been, it is certain that Napoleon's refusal to take his brother's place must ever be a source of satisfaction to the people of Bordentown and the rest of the country.

As a proof that Joseph Bonaparte had had enough of royalty, and not enough of New Jersey, it is stated that a delegation of prominent men from Mexico, which country was then in a very disturbed condition, came to him during his residence at Bordentown, and offered him the throne of Mexico. In making answer to this proposition, our ex-king did not hesitate a moment. He told the delegation, that, having already worn two crowns, he desired never again to wear another. The old fable of the fox which had lost its tail did not probably come into his mind; but if it had, he might well have spoken of it to his Mexican visitors.

After years had elapsed without any attempt on the part of European powers to arrest him, our ex-king, Joseph, began to feel safe, and he made a visit to England. He returned to America, but went back again, and died in Italy in 1844, having given to New Jersey the peculiar and unique position of being the only State in the Union which ever numbered among her citizens the owner of a royal crown and regal robes.

To be sure, there is nothing in this for the people of a republican State to be proud of; but New Jersey may be allowed to say that there never was a royal person who was of less injury to the people among whom he dwelt than her ex-king at Bordentown, and she may add that there have been very few of his class who have been of as much advantage to his neighbors.

THE DEY, THE BEY, AND SOME JERSEY
SAILORS.

NEW JERSEY is very intimate with the ocean. For nearly the whole of her length, from Cape May to Sandy Hook, the waves of the Atlantic roll and roar. Wherever one may be in this State, it is not necessary to travel very far in order to smell the fresh sea air.

It is true that but few of the great commercial vessels leave and arrive at the ports of New Jersey, and that the presence of naval vessels in her waters is due to the fact that she is part owner of the Bay of New York; but it is also true, that, although she has not sent forth ships to fight the battles of her country upon the ocean wave, she has sent out to command those ships some of the best-known men who have ever worn the American naval uniform.

One of the first occasions in which our naval vessels played a part in foreign waters was of a rather romantic nature, though not particularly calculated to raise our country's flag in our own estimation or that of other nations.

It was at the end of the eighteenth century, when we had begun to trade in various parts of the world, that our merchant vessels sailing on the Mediterranean were greatly molested by the pirates of what was called the Barbary Coast. The half-civilized and warlike people of Tripoli, Algiers, Tunis, and Morocco, had long been in the habit of sending out their armed vessels to prey upon the ships of all civilized countries; and when American ships entered the Mediterranean, they soon found out the state of affairs. Several vessels were captured, and the crews were sent on shore and imprisoned or enslaved.

Nearly all the European maritime powers had defended their commerce against these savage pirates, not by great guns and vessels of war, but by humbly paying tribute. Every year these great nations sent money and gifts to the Dey of Algiers, the Bey of Tunis, and the other rascals; and in consideration of this tribute, their vessels were graciously allowed to sail on the Mediterranean without molestation.

It was not long before the government of the United States saw very plainly that it must pay tribute, conquer the Barbary States, or quietly submit to the capture of all American merchantmen which might sail into the Mediterranean. The easiest thing to do was to pay the tribute; and as the other civilized nations did this, the United States followed their example.

In the year 1800 a United States vessel bearing the name of "George Washington," and commanded by William Bainbridge, a Jerseyman who had been at sea ever since he was fourteen years old, sailed to Algiers, carrying on board the ship which bore the name of the great man who had made his country free and independent of the most powerful nation of the earth, the tribute which was annually due from the United States to an African sovereign, the Dey of Algiers.

This commission of the United States vessel seemed more humiliating from the fact that our country had just come out of a war with France, in which our frigate "Constellation" had defeated and captured one of the vessels of that great naval power. But we had agreed to pay for the privilege of trading in the Mediterranean, and, although the countries of the Barbary Coast had no more right in that sea than Spain, France, or Italy, they chose to assert their right, and we had acknowledged it.

When Bainbridge had arrived at Algiers, and had handed over the tribute which he had brought, he supposed that his business was over, and prepared to sail away; but the Dey, who was a potentate accustomed to ask for what he wanted and to get it, informed the United States commander that he wished to send him upon an errand.

These Barbary powers were all subject to the great head of the Mohammedan nations, the Sultan of Turkey; and the Dey desired to send an ambassador to his imperial master, and as the "George Washington" was about to sail, he determined to make use of her.

When Captain Bainbridge was informed that the Dey commanded him to take the ambassador to Constantinople, he very naturally declined, and thereupon a great hubbub arose. The Dey informed Bainbridge, that, as the United States paid him tribute, its people were his slaves; they were bound, as were his other subjects, to obey his commands, and to do what he told them without hesitation or question. If they were not his slaves, why did they come here, meekly bearing money and other gifts to their master?

All this had no effect in convincing Captain Bainbridge that he was a slave of the Dey of Algiers, and bound to go upon his errands; but there was an American consul there, and he saw that the matter was very serious indeed. The harbor was commanded by forts mounted with heavy guns, and if these were brought to bear upon the "George Washington," she would certainly be blown to pieces without much chance of defending herself; and, moreover, such a conflict would surely bring about a war with Algiers, and it was not at all desirable that an American officer, bound upon friendly business, should provoke war between his country and another.

This reason was a very bitter dose for Captain Bainbridge; but after consideration he found himself obliged to take it. If he refused, there would be a

United States ship the less; and he knew not how
many American ships, now sailing without fear upon
the Mediterranean, might be seized and burned, and
their crews thrown into horrible slavery. He had no
right to precipitate anything of this sort, and consequently, under protest, he agreed to take the Algerine
ambassador to Constantinople. But this was not all the
high-minded Dey demanded. He insisted that when
the "George Washington" sailed out of the harbor,
she should sail, not as a United States vessel, but as
a ship of Algiers, and that she should carry on the
mainmast, where generally floated the stars and stripes,
the Algerine flag, while he kindly consented that the
flag of her own country might float from the foremast.
It was as difficult to refuse this second demand as it
was the first, and so the "George Washington" went
out of Algiers with the pirate's flag proudly floating
from its mainmast.

As soon as he got out of sight of land, Bainbridge
hauled down the Algerine flag and put up his own;
but this was a very small satisfaction and not particularly honorable.

When the "George Washington" reached Constantinople, she created a sensation. Never before in the
waters of the Golden Horn had the stars and stripes
been seen, and the people of the city could not imagine where this strange ship came from. Some of
these people had heard of America and the United
States, but they knew of it only in a vague and misty
way, very much as we understand some parts of the
interior of China. If Captain Bainbridge had told

them he was from New Jersey, he might as well have told them he came from the moon.

But the Americans were very well received in Constantinople, and the officers of the government were glad to welcome them and do them honor. Captain Bainbridge and the Turkish admiral became very good friends; and when the latter heard how the former had been treated at Algiers, he condemned the insolent Dey, and laid the matter before the Turkish Government. In consequence of this, Bainbridge was given a paper, signed by the Sultan, which would protect him thereafter from any such disrespectful treatment from any of the minor Mohammedan powers. When Captain Bainbridge had enjoyed all the Turkish hospitality his duties permitted him to receive, he sailed from Constantinople and again entered the port of Algiers. The Dey was glad to see him come back, for he had some more business for him; and our Jersey captain was soon informed that he must sail away again on another errand for his Barbary master. But this time the Barbary master was very much astonished, for Bainbridge peremptorily refused to do anything of the kind.

Now the blood of the Dey boiled hot, and he vowed that if the "George Washington" did not immediately sail forth upon his service, he would declare war upon this miserable little country which owned it, and he would put the commander and crew of the ship in chains, and clap them into dungeons. But Bainbridge did not turn pale, nor did he tremble. He simply pulled from his pocket the paper which he had received from the Sultan, and allowed the furious Dey to glance over it. When the raving pirate read the words of his imperial master, all the fury and the courage went out of him, and he became as meek and humble as if he had been somebody come to pay a tribute to himself. He received Bainbridge as a friend and an equal, and, from commanding and threatening him, became so gracious, and made so many offers of service and friendship, that Bainbridge decided to take advantage of this auspicious change of temper.

Not long before, the French consul at Algiers had been seized and imprisoned, together with all the Frenchmen who were doing business in that place; for, so long as people belonged to a country which was a great way off, the Dey considered himself an all-powerful ruler, who could do what he pleased with them without fear of their far-away government. Bainbridge determined to try to do something for these poor men; and when he again met the smiling and pleasant Dey, he urged their release. The paper which Bainbridge received from the Sultan must have been written in very strong terms; for, although the demand of the American captain was a heavy one, the Dey agreed to it, and when the "George Washington" sailed from Algiers, she carried away all the Frenchmen who had been living there.

Bainbridge was not at all satisfied with this Algerine business; and when he reported the affair to the authorities at home, he requested that he might never again be sent to carry tribute to Algiers unless he could deliver it from the mouths of his cannon.

The next year the Bashaw of Tripoli, who had had
no tribute from the United States, began to be very
uneasy in his mind because he did not fare so well
as the other Barbary potentates, to whom money and
merchandise were delivered every year. He accordingly spoke up in defense of his rights. It is not
likely that he knew where the United States was,
what sort of a country it was, or how large or how
small its army and navy might be. He knew that
the Americans were miserable, humble people, who
paid tribute to the Bey and the Dey, and he could
see no particular reason why they should not pay it
to the Bashaw. Consequently he wrote a letter to the
President of the United States, in which he expressed
his views very pointedly, and informed him, that, if
proper arrangements were not made in six months, he
would destroy all the American ships on the Mediterranean, and declare war against the United States.

Strange to say, a thrill of terror did not run through
the government of the United States; and six months
passed without any notice having been taken of this
impertinent communication. Thereupon the Bashaw
cut down the flag pole in front of the American consul's office at Tripoli, and commenced the great work
of annihilating the United States of America. He
began on the small American trading vessels which
he found along the Barbary Coast, intending probably,
when his convenience would permit, to sail out upon
the Atlantic, find the United States, and help himself
to the treasures which its government had so disrespectfully declined to hand over to him. The ex-

ample of the Bashaw had a great effect upon the Dey
and the Bey and the sub-Sultan; and Algiers, Tunis,
and Morocco also informed the President of the United
States that they were going to war with him if he did
not immediately promise to pay tribute more regularly
and in articles of better quality.

But the United States was getting tired of this sort
of thing, and determined, no matter what the other
civilized powers chose to do, that no more tribute
should be paid by it to these insolent pirates.   Consequently our government informed the mighty mon-
archs of the Barbary Coast that it was quite ready for
war, and sent four ships to the Mediterranean, one of
which, the "Essex," was commanded by Bainbridge.

But the fleet did not do very much on this expedition, and the war with North Africa dragged considerably.   Bainbridge came back to America, and after
a time returned in command of the "Philadelphia."
There was a small squadron with him, but he sailed
faster than the other vessels, and reached the Mediterranean alone.   Here he overhauled a Moorish vessel which had captured an American brig under a
commission from Morocco.   Having rescued the American vessel, the crew of which were prisoners in the
pirates' hold, the "Philadelphia" took the Moorish
vessel as a prize to Gibraltar, and then started out
again to see what could be done to humble the port
of Tripoli.

In this undertaking our Jerseyman did not meet with
good fortune.   In chasing a Tripolitan vessel which
was discovered near the harbor, the "Philadelphia"

ran upon a reef, and there stuck fast. Everything was done that could be done to get her off; even the cannon were thrown overboard to lighten her, but it was of no use. She was hard and fast; and when the people of Tripoli found out what had happened, their gunboats came out of the harbor, and the "Philadelphia" was captured, and all on board, including Bainbridge, were made prisoners. They were taken to Tripoli, and there remained in captivity nineteen months. Now the soul of the Bey swelled high in his bosom as he smiled at this attempt of the little country across the ocean to resist his power.

The Tripolitans found that they had gained a great prize in the "Philadelphia," that fine war ship, which seemed to have been left on the reef as a present to them. After a good deal of work, they towed her into the harbor close to the town, where they repaired her leaks, and put her in order to use against their enemies the Americans, who did not know how to keep a good thing when they had it. When Commodore Preble came, six months afterwards, to blockade the port of Tripoli, he discovered that the "Philadelphia" was nearly ready for sea; and, to prevent the disaster of having a United States ship with United States cannon bear down upon them, he determined to destroy the "Philadelphia," if possible, and an excellent plan for the purpose was devised. A small vessel called the "Intrepid," which had been captured some time previously, was manned with a crew of over eighty men, commanded by Lieutenant Decatur, who, years after, finished the Algerine war.

This brave little vessel sailed into the harbor as if she had been an ordinary merchantman, and managed to drift down close to the fine frigate which the Tripolitans had snatched from their blundering enemy. The crew on board the "Philadelphia" did not suspect the character of the little vessel which came so close to them, until she was made fast, and more than eighty men sprang up from the places where they had been lying concealed on deck, and swarmed over the side of the frigate.

Among these was a young sailor, Lawrence, from Burlington, N.J., who had begun life early, having been a midshipman when he was only sixteen years old. When Commodore Preble asked for volunteers to go on this expedition to snatch from the hands of the pirates the prize which they thought they had won, Lawrence was one of the first volunteers, and acted as second in command of this expedition.

The fight was not long. Many of the turbaned crew jumped overboard, and the others were quickly subdued. It would have been a grand thing if Decatur and his gallant sailors could have carried off the "Philadelphia," and have taken her out to the squadron. But this was absolutely impossible. Her foremast had been cut down in order to lighten her so that she could be floated off the reef, and many of her sails were wanting. Knowing that the vessel would not be found in sailing trim, Preble had issued positive orders that no attempt should be made to capture her, but that she should be burned.

The cannon from the town and from the war vessels in the port now began to fire; but the men with Decatur and Lawrence knew exactly what they had to do, everything having been carefully arranged beforehand. They went to work without losing a minute, and set fire to the frigate in many places. The flames and the smoke spread so rapidly that some of them had hardly time to get out of the hold. Lieutenant Lawrence found he could not get on deck the way he came down, and was obliged to run along the hold and climb up forward. As quickly as possible every one jumped on board the "Intrepid," and, without rely-

ing entirely on their sails to enable them to get away,
they put out sixteen great oars, which were pulled with
a will by three or four men to each oar.

Now the whole harbor of Tripoli was in wild com-
motion. The Americans stopped rowing for a moment
to give three great cheers, and soon cannon shot were
flying fast and furious after the retreating little vessel.
But only one of them touched her, and that passed
through a sail without doing much damage; and she
rowed until her sails caught the wind, and then went
out of the harbor, and returned in triumph to the
squadron.

Soon after they had left the " Philadelphia." that
great vessel, with her hull blazing and the flames crac-
kling and climbing up her masts, took it upon herself,
in these last minutes of her existence, to strike a blow
for the flag of her country. Possibly suspecting that
some attempt might be made to rescue the ship they
had captured, the Tripolitans had loaded all her cannon
so as to be ready to fire upon any vessel that might
approach her. As the fire spread over her hull, the
time came when the " Philadelphia " could do something for herself; and when the guns were hot enough,
she let fly a broadside into the town, and then another
one among the shipping. How much damage she did,
we do not know; but the soul of the Bashaw ceased
to swell as he heard the roar of her last broadsides,
and beheld her burning fragments scattered over the
waters of the harbor.

But when the Bashaw of Tripoli imprisoned Bainbridge, and even after he had seen the frigate he had

captured disappear in flames and smoke, he found he
was not yet rid of Jersey sailors. Some months afterwards, when Commodore Preble was still off the Barbary Coast, there was a vessel in the squadron called
the "Nautilus," which was commanded by a young
Jerseyman named Somers. He was a brave sailor, and
had already distinguished himself on several occasions.

Fighting the Bey was a good deal like trying to get
at a rat in a hole, and, although there were some good
fights in the Tripolitan waters, the fleet did not meet
with much success at first. But the Americans were
very anxious to do something effective, for at that
time Bainbridge and his crew were imprisoned in the
town, and no one knew what hardships and cruelties
they might be enduring.

After much consideration it was thought that a good
way to strike a decisive blow would be to send a vessel loaded with shells and gunpowder into the harbor
of Tripoli by night, and explode her there. This might
result, it was thought, in the destruction of the forts
and ships, and possibly part of the town, and so ter-
rify the Bey that he would come to terms. Lieutenant Somers, who had been foremost in contriving this
project, volunteered to command the expedition. The
whole affair was so extremely dangerous that no one
was ordered to take part in it, and all those who wished
to go went of their own free will.

The "Intrepid," the small vessel on which Decatur
and Lawrence had sailed to burn the "Philadelphia,"
was still with the fleet, and this was heavily loaded
with explosives of all kinds. The plan was, that after

nightfall the "Intrepid" should be sailed as near as possible to the town, and that, after lighting the slow match which communicated with the terrible cargo, those on board should take to two small boats which they had in tow, and row out of the harbor as fast as possible, leaving there the "Intrepid" to hurl fire and destruction into the enemy's strongholds.

Before Somers started out on this perilous voyage, he addressed the few men who were to accompany him, and told them that he wanted no one to go who would not be willing to blow himself up rather than be captured. It was well known that the Tripolitans were short of ammunition, and if they suspected what sort of a vessel it was which floated by night into the harbor, they would board her and capture her, if it should be possible, and thus gain possession of a great quantity of powder and shell. Rather than that this should happen, Somers told his men that he would blow up the little vessel with all on board, if the enemy should take it. But no man flinched; and after they had all taken leave of their friends on the fleet, as if they had been going to execution, the "Intrepid" slowly sailed away into the harbor, and it was not long before she was lost to view in the mists of the night.

But after a time it became apparent to those on the American fleet that she was not lost to view to those in the harbor, for the guns of the fort began to fire on her. Everybody who had a glass kept it fixed on that part of the harbor where it was supposed Somers and his little vessel must be, and in course of time they saw a light rapidly moving as if some one were carrying a lantern from one end of the vessel to the other. Then in less than a minute there was a blaze and a roar, and the whole harbor of Tripoli was lighted up as if there had been an explosion of fireworks. Sparks and fiery fragments flew into the air, and the waters seemed to be shaken as if by an earthquake. Then all was silent and dark.

Of course, the "Intrepid" had blown up, but how or why nobody on the fleet could know; nor did Somers and his brave crew ever come back to tell them. Some people thought, and still think, that the "Intrepid" was about to be captured, and that Somers carried out his resolution to blow up the vessel under him rather than allow it to be taken. Others suppose that a red-hot cannon ball from one of the forts may have set the vessel on fire; but the truth no one knows. We only know that this brave young Jerseyman went out to his fate determined to do his duty, no matter what happened, and that he died in doing it.

SEA FIGHTS WITH A NOBLER FOE.

THE war with the Barbary pirates was all sorts of a war. Sometimes there was fighting, and sometimes there was none; and after Bainbridge was released, he was engaged part of the time in the mercantile service until the war with Great Britain broke out in 1812. Early in this war, Bainbridge took command of the "Constitution," the same vessel which, a few months before, had had a fight with the "Guerrière," in which the latter was captured. It is a good deal better, sometimes, to fight with a strong enemy who will stand up bravely in front of you, and let you see what he is, than to contend with a mean little one who is continually getting out of the way and bobbing up at unexpected places, and making it very difficult either to get at him or to know when he is going to get at you. Consequently there is no doubt that Bainbridge much preferred to do battle with the naval power of Great Britain rather than with the pirates of Barbary.

He sailed down the coast of South America, and there he met the "Java," a British frigate. He had a hard fight and a long fight, and the end of it was that the "Java" hauled down her flag after having a great portion of her crew killed and wounded; and, as she was so thoroughly shattered and broken up by the guns of the "Constitution," the victors could not take her home as a prize, but were obliged to burn her.

If any one had been inclined to deride the Jersey-man at sea, after what had happened to Bainbridge in the Mediterranean, he changed his opinion after the affair with the "Java." In fact, a gold medal was voted to the gallant captain by Congress. When the war with Great Britain was over, Bainbridge took a squadron to the Mediterranean to try his hand again at protecting American commerce, and humbling the pirates; but fortune did not favor him this time, for Decatur had already settled the matter with the Dey, the Bey, and the rest of them, and peace was declared before Bainbridge arrived on the scene. Our Jersey sailor did not do any more fighting, but he held high positions in our navy, and died an honored commodore.

Years after the affair with the "Philadelphia," when war had begun between the United States and Great Britain, there was a great chance for America to show what she could do on the sea. Then the fighting men in ships were more important to the country than the fighting men on shore; and Captain Lawrence, our fighting sailor from Burlington, showed himself among the foremost of our naval heroes.

Very early in the war he was in command of the "Hornet," a snappish vessel with more stings than one, and while cruising in South American waters he met the British man-of-war "Peacock." Now, when a hornet and a peacock quarrel, lively times are likely to ensue, and so it happened in this case.

The two vessels began by endeavoring to get into favorable positions, each anxious to rake the deck of the other. The "Peacock" did not spread her tail, but she spread her sail, and the "Hornet" buzzed this way and that, with her stings ready for action as soon as the proper moment should arrive. When at last they actually began to fight, the battle was a terrible one, such as was possible only in those days of wooden ships. But a short distance apart, they poured into each other heavy shot and small shot; musketry and cannon cracked and roared, while the clouds of smoke nearly hid the vessels from each other. This tremendous bombardment lasted about a quarter of an hour, and at the end of that time the "Peacock" struck her colors and surrendered. The captain and a good many of the crew had been killed, and the vessel was in such a demolished condition that there was not time to get all the prisoners and the wounded on board the "Hornet." The officers and men of the American vessel labored hard to save those on board their unfortunate enemy; but the "Peacock" sank before this could be entirely accomplished, and several of the British sailors, with three of those from the "Hornet," sank with her.

Captain Lawrence was not only a brave man, but he was a very kind one. He treated the officers and crew of the "Peacock" so well, even providing them with clothes (for they had no time to bring anything from their own vessel), that when the prisoners reached

New York, the officers publicly thanked him in a paper which they drew up and signed. This victory, following our other brilliant exploits at sea, gave Lawrence great fame both here and abroad.

A few months after the battle between the "Hornet" and the "Peacock," Lawrence was again the hero of a great sea fight. The coast of New England was blockaded by a British fleet, and in the harbor of Boston lay the frigate "Chesapeake," commanded by Captain Lawrence. He had been recently appointed to this vessel, and in fact had been in command only ten days when he received a challenge to fight a naval duel.

This proposition came from the captain of the British frigate "Shannon," one of the blockading fleet, about the same size and strength as the "Chesapeake." The British captain sent a very polite letter to Captain Lawrence; for when people propose to fight duels, whether on land or sea, they are always extremely courteous before they begin to try to kill each other. The British captain said, that, as he understood the "Chesapeake" was now ready to go to sea, he would like her to come out and fight the "Shannon" for the honor of their respective flags. He offered the American captain choice of fighting ground inside of certain limits, and promised that the rest of the British fleet should keep far away, so that Captain Lawrence need have no fear of being troubled by any vessel except the "Shannon."

When Captain Lawrence read this challenge, he was as willing to go out and fight the duel as the British captain was anxious to have him do so; but he knew that his vessel was not nearly so well prepared as was the "Shannon." The British ship had been at sea for a long time, she was manned by a crew of brave sailors, and her captain was well acquainted with his ship and his men.

The case was very different with the "Chesapeake." Lawrence had been on board scarcely long enough to find out what sort of a ship she was, but he had been on board long enough to discover that her crew was a very poor one. Many of them were Portuguese, they had not been well drilled, and, worse than that, they did not want to fight. Few of them had been in the service long enough to have a taste for naval warfare; and if they had had their way, they would have let the "Shannon" lie outside until her captain grew gray, before they would go out and accept his challenge. The harbor was much more to their mind.

But Captain Lawrence had no such idea. He accepted the challenge without hesitation, and prepared to go out and fight the duel. He would have been glad enough if he had had a good crew, but he would do his best with the crew he had. He put his ship in fighting trim, and his men in the best order possible, and early on a summer afternoon the "Chesapeake" went out to meet the "Shannon," which was boldly flying the flag of St. George.

In those days, when men-of-war, as well as all other ships, were sailing vessels, the tactics of naval combats were very different from what they are now. Each of the commanders of vessels was obliged to think, not only of what his enemy was about, but what the wind was about. A steamer can take what position she pleases; she can steam far away from her enemy, or she can use her long-range guns, or dash down upon her to break in her sides with her ram. But in the old sailing times, maneuvers were very much more difficult, and if the winds ever desired to stop a sea fight, it often happened that they could do it simply by dying away themselves.

The two ships sailed this way and that, each trying to get a position which would be good for herself and bad for the other; and at last, when they were very close, so near that their captains might have talked with each other, their cannon began to speak. From their mouths came rolling of thunder. From each ship, volleys of great shot swept the decks of the other, while the rattle of musketry became incessant. This tremendous fire was kept up for nearly ten minutes, and in this short time the "Chesapeake" lost nearly one hundred men, killed and wounded, on her upper deck.

Still she had the best of the fight, for in a few minutes she would have taken a position in which she could have raked the decks of the enemy. But unfortunately some of her rigging was shot away, and she could not take advantage of the wind, and did not obey her helm. Nothing could be worse than this; for, with sails flapping wildly in the wind, precision of sailing, so necessary in a sea fight, was absolutely impossible.

But not only was the "Chesapeake" unable to take the position she wanted, but she could not get out

of the way, and she drifted against the "Shannon;"
and the rigging of the two vessels became entangled,
with the "Chesapeake" exposed to the full fire of the
guns of the other ship. In this case there was only
one thing to be done, and Captain Lawrence was the
brave man to do it. He must board the "Shannon,"
and he and his men must fight her captain and his
men hand to hand. There was no use trying to fight
any longer with the "Chesapeake's" cannon.

Instantly Lawrence ordered the boarders to be called
on deck, and he was ready to put himself at their head
and dash on board the "Shannon." He was slightly
wounded, but he did not care for that. But now
came another misfortune. The man who should have
called the boarders to action by the roll of the drum
was not on duty, and the bugler was ordered to sound
the call. He was so frightened by this awful fight
that he ran and hid himself, and when he was pulled
out from his retreat, he had not breath enough to blow
his bugle. Some of the men were sent below to shout
for the boarders and call them on deck, — a very slow
procedure at such a time; but before any of them
arrived, the brave Lawrence was stretched upon the
deck by a musket ball.

The captain of the "Chesapeake" was not immediately killed, but he was mortally wounded; and when
he was carried below, he showed that, near death as
he was, he was still the bravest man on board. He
thought nothing of himself, he thought only of his
country and his ship; and his last orders were, "Don't
give up the ship. Fight her till she sinks."

But it was not much use trying to fight the "Shannon" any longer; there were no officers on the deck of the "Chesapeake," except two midshipmen, and the British captain saw that he had a good chance to board his enemy. So his crew were soon clambering over the sides of the American vessel. Some wounded officers rushed up from below to help repel this attack. Many of the American sailors fought bravely even at these great odds; but some of the crew, especially the Portuguese, basely deserted their comrades and hurried below. The fight on the deck of the "Chesapeake" was not a long one; and very soon the stars and stripes were hauled down from her masthead, and the British colors hoisted in their place.

So ended the great duel between the "Chesapeake" and the "Shannon," and the last words of the brave

Lawrence were never forgotten. "Don't give up the ship" became the watchword of the navy.

After this bloody sea fight, which lasted only fifteen minutes, but in which nearly two hundred and fifty men were killed and wounded, the "Shannon" sailed away for Halifax, taking with her the "Chesapeake," with the dead body of its brave commander on board. When the two vessels entered the harbor, Lawrence lay upon the quarter-deck, wrapped in the great flag of the "Chesapeake," while all the men on the British vessels in the harbor manned their yards, and shouted a wild welcome to the victorious "Shannon." But the flag which floated from the masthead of the British frigate held no more honorable position than that which covered the dead body of the American hero.

THE STORY OF THE TELEGRAPH AND THE STEAMBOAT.

IT will always be a source of commendable pride to the people of New Jersey, that their State was never backward in the political, social, or mechanical progress of this country. In fact, several of the most important steps in great movements for popular good have been made upon the soil of the State.

Among the claims to preëminence which New Jersey can make in this respect is the claim that the first telegraphic message that was ever transmitted through a wire was sent at the Iron Works at Speedwell, near Morristown, at which place Professor Morse and Mr. Vail, son of the proprietor of the works, were making experiments with the telegraph. The first public message was sent more than six years later from Washington to Baltimore; but the message at Speedwell stands first, in the point of priority, of all the dispatches by magnetic telegraph which the world has known.

When Professor Morse conceived the idea of communicating between distant points by means of electricity, he was not able to carry out experiments for himself, and having made the acquaintance of Alfred Vail, son of the proprietor of the Iron Works at Speedwell, he gave up his business as a portrait painter and went to Speedwell, where he and Mr. Vail worked hard in experimenting with the new invention. At last, when they thought they had brought it to such a point that they could make practical use of it, they determined to try to send a message through three miles of wire. If that could be done, they believed they could send one to any distance desirable.

Currents of electricity had been sent through long lengths of wire by Mr. Morse in previous experiments, but in these cases nothing more was attempted than signals; no words or message had been sent, and the proposed experiment, therefore, was of great importance. Its success or failure meant success or failure to the magnetic telegraph.

The upper story of a house on the grounds of the Iron Works was one very large room, and round the walls of this they stretched their three miles of wire, until the room was encircled by lines of wire, one above another, but nowhere touching. At one end of this wire was placed a telegraphic instrument, and at the other, another; and with great anxiety, although with strong faith in the success of their work, Mr. Vail sent to Mr. Morse the first real telegraphic message, which ran thus: "A patient waiter is no loser."

The house in which this first message was sent is still standing, near the Whippany River, not far out of Morristown. Alfred Vail and Mr. Morse, assisted by the advice of Professor Joseph Henry, superintendent of the Smithsonian Institution at Washington, continued to work upon the telegraph at Speedwell; and as Mr. Vail furnished the capital, and did a great deal of the most important mechanical work, a large portion of the credit for this wonderful invention is due to him; and the whole system of telegraphy which now encircles and animates the world may be said to have sprung from the Iron Works near Morristown.

Another great invention, as important as the telegraph, made its first appearance before the world in New Jersey. In the frozen waters about the North Pole, on the rivers of Africa, in the seas of China and Japan, on the stormy ocean about Cape Horn, and in almost all navigable waters of the world, are steamboats and steamships,—floating palaces on rivers and lakes, steam yachts and great Atlantic liners, swift war cruisers and line-of-battle ships like floating forts of iron and steel; but the first vessel which was ever propelled by steam paddled its way along the Delaware River, and was made in New Jersey.

In 1787 John Fitch, who was a native of Connecticut, but who lived at that time in Trenton, N.J., where he had been a clock maker and manufacturer of arms, constructed a boat which was moved through the water by means of a steam engine on board. He had long been working on this invention, making experiments, and endeavoring to obtain assistance from people with money. He had applied to Congress to give him the exclusive right to the great results of his work if he should be successful; but this aid was refused.

New Jersey, Delaware, and Pennsylvania, however, gave him the right for fourteen years to propel vessels upon the waters of those States; and thus encouraged he built the first steamboat. This little vessel was imperfect in many ways, and its highest speed was four miles an hour; but still it was a steamboat, and it was the first that man had ever seen. Of course, it attracted a good deal of attention; and after it had been proved that it could move without sails or oars, and that it was not dangerous, people began to believe in it, and a steamboat company was organized by Fitch. Another boat was built, which carried passengers who paid their fare, and afterwards a larger boat was constructed, in the hope that a good passenger traffic might be established.

We cannot wonder that there should have been a desire among enterprising people to establish some better method of transportation in travel than existed in the early days of New Jersey. At first the only roads in the State were narrow paths, sometimes more than fifty miles long, but only wide enough for the easy passage of a man on horseback: After that, better roads gradually came into use; and in the beginning of the eighteenth century there was a "stage wagon," intended for the carriage of merchandise, not passengers, which made a trip every two weeks from Perth Amboy to Philadelphia. This was considered as a great public convenience; because, before that, there was no regular method of shipping merchandise from New York to Philadelphia, except by sea.

After a time, stage wagons, which carried passengers, began to run in some parts of New Jersey; and in 1750 a grand stage line was established, intended especially for the transportation of travelers. In an advertisement the proprietor of this line announced to all persons "who have occasion to transport themselves, goods, stores, or merchandise from New York to Philadelphia," that he would take them in "forty-eight hours less than by any other line," and he promised to "use the people in the best manner." It is stated that this trip by land and water between New York and Philadelphia lasted seven or eight days, although it now seems almost impossible to travel so slowly.

Sixteen years afterward, a new and improved line of stage wagons was established, which were faster and very much more comfortable than any which had yet been known. They were actually mounted on springs, and it was promised that the trip would be made in two days in summer, and three days in winter. These stagecoaches were so much swifter than anything else of the kind ever known in the State, that they were called "flying machines."

Fifteen years afterward, the price of conveyance between New York and Philadelphia on one of these "flying machines" was forty shillings in gold or silver for each passenger, and as much for each hundred and fifty pounds of baggage.

The mail facilities in those days were as poor as the methods for transportation; and we can get an

idea of the postal arrangements from an extract from
a New York paper published in 1704, which states,
"In the pleasant month of May, the last storm put
our Pennsylvania post a week behind, and has not yet
com'd in." But although this was rather slow communication, New Jersey was better off than many of
the civilized communities of the day; for she had a
regular postal system, which had been invented by
Colonel John Hamilton.

Colonel Hamilton's system was considered so good,
that the British Government gave him a patent for it,
and adopted it for the mother country, it being considered much better than the system then in use.
The mails were generally carried in canvas bags by
men on horseback; and this method of transportation
was known as the "express," as a horse and his rider
could go much more rapidly than even the best "flying machines." Mail service in New Jersey greatly
improved before the end of the century.

But it was very hard to persuade the public to en-
courage Fitch's new enterprise, even although it promised cheaper and more rapid transportation than any
methods in use; and of course it was still harder,
from the fact that the new steamboats had not yet
gone faster than a sailing vessel with a good breeze.
And so, notwithstanding the value of a system of navigation by which vessels could be made to move whether
there was a breeze or not, and in any direction no
matter how the wind was blowing, there was very little support to the new steamboat, and the enterprise
was so unprofitable that it was given up.

Nearly ten years after Fitch's largest steamboat had been sold as a piece of useless property, Robert Fulton made a steamboat which ran on the Hudson River at the rate of five miles an hour; and after this the practicability of steam navigation began to be slowly acknowledged. But the waters of New Jersey were the first which were ever ruffled by the paddles of a steamboat.

New Jersey has another claim to distinction in connection with steam navigation, for at the Speedwell Iron Works were manufactured some of the larger portions of the machinery of the "Savannah," the first steamship which ever crossed the ocean.

NEW JERSEY AND THE LAND OF GOLD.

THERE was another famous American sailor who came out of New Jersey, who was perhaps of as much value to his country as any other naval commander, although he was not the hero of any great sea fights.

This was Robert F. Stockton, who was born in Princeton, and who entered the navy early in life. He became an excellent officer and a great fighter. His disposition to do battle showed itself not only in leading men into action, but in doing a great deal of fighting himself. He distinguished himself in several naval combats during the war with Algiers. He commanded the "Spitfire" during this war, and, besides taking one of the enemy's vessels in an ordinary naval combat, he captured an Algerine brig, one might almost say, with his own hands. With as many men as a small boat could carry, he left his vessel, rowed to this brig, and at the head of his bold sailors boarded her, vanquished the crew, and carried her off as a prize.

He was afterwards transferred to a larger vessel, and was stationed for a time at Gibraltar. There was a very bad feeling at that time between the American naval officers and those of Great Britain. The War of 1812 was over; but the British were not inclined to treat the officers of the United States Navy with the respect which the latter thought was due to them. Stockton was not a man to stand still and allow himself to be treated disrespectfully; and whenever he received anything that seemed like an insult from a British officer, he was ready to fight that officer, whoever he might be. It is said that at one time he challenged all the officers in Gibraltar to meet him in single combat, one after another, and he actually did engage in duels with several of them.

During the British war and the Algerine war, Stockton distinguished himself in various ways, both on land and sea. But in 1821 he undertook a very important enterprise in Africa. Many naval vessels had gone from the United States to Africa, but none of them on an errand such as this. Our gallant Jersey captain did not sail to pay tribute, bombard cities, sink vessels, humble African potentates, or to shed African blood; he went on an errand of charity and humanity.

He sailed from America in the interests of the Colonization Society, and his object was to make arrangements on the west coast of Africa for the establishment of a colony, to be composed of negroes who had been slaves in the United States, but who had obtained their freedom. There were many humane people in the United States who believed that the negroes who had been set free from slavery would be much happier and more likely to prosper in their native land, or in the land of their ancestors, than in the United States.

In company with an agent of this society, Stockton
sailed for the west coast of Africa in command of an
armed schooner called the "Alligator;" and when he
arrived at his destination, he took upon himself nearly
all the difficult work of selecting territory suitable for
the purposes desired, of buying land from the savage
natives, of making them understand the character of
the settlers who were coming to Africa and of the
powerful nation who intended to protect them. He
made treaties of commerce and friendship with the
ignorant Africans, who, until he came, scarcely knew
what was meant by a treaty.

The performance of these complicated and difficult
duties required a man of courage and diplomatic ability,
who could take things as they came, and who was
always ready to act promptly in sudden emergencies.
Stockton proved himself to be that man, and he established in the native land of the negro a country to
which the Africans who had once been slaves in the
United States might freely go, carrying with them all
that they had learned of civilization in this country,
and where they might live without fear of reënslave-
ment by the warlike tribes, whose principal business
in life then was to capture their fellow-countrymen,
and sell them into slavery.

This new country, which was called Liberia, was at
first a colony of the United States. It grew and prospered, and in 1847 it became an independent nation,
and soon after was recognized as such by Great Britain and the United States; and since then it has
made treaties with most of the European countries.

Thus was established the new nation of Liberia, and it is not likely that there was a man in the United States who could have accomplished this great work better than the fighting sailor from Princeton.

After having finished the Liberian business on land, Stockton did some work at sea more in the line of a naval commander. While sailing along the coast, the "Alligator" was sighted by a Portuguese war vessel, the "Marianna Flora," who mistook her for a pirate, and determined to capture her. But when the "Marianna" got near enough, and opened fire on the supposed pirate, she found that the work she had undertaken was very different from what she had expected. To speak figuratively, the "Alligator" lashed her tail, opened her jaws, and began to fight with such fury, that in twenty minutes the "Marianna" was beaten and captured. Stockton put her under the command of one of his own officers with an American crew, and sent her away as a prize to America.

The government of Portugal, when it heard what had happened, declared, that, as their country and the United States were not at war, our Jersey sailor had no right to take one of their vessels; but, as it was asserted on the other side that one of their vessels had first tried to take his, there seemed to be a good deal of justice in what had been done. However, the matter was settled by his exoneration from all blame in the matter, and the return of the "Marianna" to Portugal.

Some time later, the "Alligator" fell in with a French slave ship and captured her; and it is stated that the legal proceedings which followed this capture established the point of international law, that war vessels of all nations have a perfect right to capture a slave ship, wherever it may be found. This was the first step in the work of breaking up the slave trade, which was then carried on by many of the civilized nations of the world.

In later cruises, Stockton sailed about in the West Indies, capturing several slavers, and also making a vigorous war on pirates and freebooters, who at that time made the vicinity of these islands very dangerous for peaceable vessels.

In 1838 our commander was made a captain. There was no war now in which he might engage, but his mind was very busily occupied in regard to the proper construction of war vessels. In 1841 the United States Navy did not possess a single steamship. They were all old-style sailing vessels. Several steamers had been planned: one had blown up, and two others were still on the stocks. But Captain Stockton did not believe that if these were finished they would be effective as vessels of war. One great reason for this was the fact that their engines were situated so near the upper deck, that a shot from an enemy might easily destroy them, and so render the vessel worthless. Another objection was that they were side-wheelers, and it would be a very easy thing for a cannon ball to knock an exposed side-wheel into a worthless condition.

Stockton's idea was to put the engines and machinery deep down in the vessel, below the water line, where it would be almost impossible to injure them, and to have the ship moved by means of a submerged screw in the stern, instead of by paddle wheels. The naval constructors and authorities opposed this new-fangled scheme; but our New Jersey sailor was an energetic man in whatever he had to do, and he fought the naval constructors as vigorously as he ever fought a pirate. Consequently he got authority from Congress to build a war ship after his own plan, and arm it with cannon, which he thought would be much better than the guns then in use in the navy.

Under Stockton's directions, there was built at Philadelphia a vessel of war, which he named the "Princeton," and which was constructed according to his plans. On her deck were two great guns of wrought iron, which were also devised by him; and each of these carried a two hundred and twenty-five pound shot,— much heavier than those then used in naval warfare.

Great public interest was excited in the "Princeton," the first steamship of our navy, and on her trial trip she was found to be an excellent seagoing vessel. She went to Washington, and there started out on an excursion, during which her great guns were to be tried. There was a very distinguished company on board,— officers of the army and navy, and several members of the Cabinet, and other guests.

It was found, however, that the ship was much superior to her great guns; for when one of them, named the "Peacemaker," was fired, it exploded, killing several people, among whom were the secretary of war, the secretary of the navy, and the father-in-law of the President; while others, including Captain Stockton, were wounded.

This terrible event shocked the whole nation; but although there were no more wrought-iron cannon made, the building of naval steamships, which began with Stockton's "Princeton," went steadily on, growing and improving, until it reached the high point shown by the swift and powerful ironclad men-of-war which now fly the stars and stripes.

In 1846 Stockton found himself on the coast of California, with the rank of commodore, and in command of a squadron. Since he had started from the United States, war had been declared with Mexico; and when he arrived, the towns of Monterey and San Francisco had been taken by Commodore Sloat, who had preceded him. A state of war exactly suited Stockton's disposition; and as there was no more immediate need of fighting on the seacoast, he organized a little army of marines and sailors from his ships, which was afterwards joined by a body of adventurers and hunters of the United States, and also by Lieutenant-Colonel Frémont, an officer of the United States Army, who had been sent into that region to explore the country, and who had already done some fighting with the little band under his command.

Los Angeles, the Mexican capital of California, was attacked and taken. Commodore Stockton now declared himself the conqueror of California, and organized a provisional government for the captured territory, appointing John C. Frémont as governor.

At the same time, however, there was another Jerseyman in the field intent upon the capture of California. This was General Stephen Kearney, an army officer who had made a wonderful march across the plains and mountains towards the coast. After he arrived on the scene, there were several battles with the Mexican forces and with the Indians; but the contest ended in a complete victory for the land forces commanded by Kearney from Newark, and the naval forces by Stockton from Princeton, under whom Frémont held his position.

But now arose a dispute between the general and the commodore. When Kearney arrived at Los Angeles, he would not recognize the authority of Frémont, who had been appointed governor by Stockton, because he considered that an army officer is higher in rank than one in the navy; and he took the governorship himself. A court-martial was convened for the purpose of deciding the question, and it was settled that Kearney was of the higher rank, and he therefore retained the governorship. But between the two Jerseymen the United States obtained the land of gold.

A year or two after this, Commodore Stockton resigned from the navy, and subsequently went to Congress as a senator from New Jersey. But although no longer in the navy, he did not cease to work for the benefit of the brave sailors he had so often commanded and led; and he obtained the passage of a bill abolishing the punishment of flogging in the navy, thus adding another great gift to his country and civilization.

When the country which had been captured from Mexico was discovered to be not only a fertile and pleasant land, but a land filled with rich treasures of gold, the true value of the gift made to the United States by our two Jerseymen became known and appreciated; and the names of Stockton and Kearney, with that of the brave Frémont, will ever be associated with that State whose principal water portal is well called the "Golden Gate."

TYPOGRAPHY BY J. S. CUSHING & CO., NORWOOD, MASS.

A BASIC LIBRARY OF NEW JERSEY HISTORY

The provision of a collection of local history materials is a responsibility of any public or school library, no matter how small, yet relatively few collections adequate to the need are to be found, especially in school libraries. This is not necessarily due to inattention on the part of the library staff. Local history materials are frequently " fugitive," published outside regular channels of the book trade, in small, quickly exhausted editions, or at a considerable price; moreover, many aspects of New Jersey history are still to be adequately documented. A surprising amount of authentic and interesting material is nevertheless available for acquisition.

Research workers and advanced students have access to such extensive collections as those at the Newark Public Library, the New Jersey Historical Society (Newark), Rutgers University (New Brunswick), Princeton University, the Stewart Collection at Glassboro State College, the Trenton Public Library, the Trenton State College Library, and the New Jersey State Library (Trenton). Young people in upper grades and high school must as a rule, however, content themselves with the materials in their local public or school library, since the special collections contain manuscript material or unreplaceable books (such as the " Authorities " referred to by Stockton) whose use must be restricted to the mature searcher.

The books listed in this " Basic Library " have, for these reasons, been selected to represent a minimum collection on early New Jersey history up to the time of the Civil War. They should be available in all public and school libraries in the state and may also provide a basis for personal buying. All these books are at present in print and can be recommended as authentic sources for the topics and period of history covered by Stockton. Biographies and works of fictions are not included, except for a select list of stories for upper grades and high school, which are needed because of the scarcity of readable factual material at this level and the heavy demand from school assignments. Nor are accounts of single towns or counties included. For a more extensive bibliography of Jerseyana, the reader may write to the Director of the Library, Trenton State College, Trenton, New Jersey.

The total collection recommended here would cost about $130 at bookstore prices.

Symbols used: Recommended for grades 4-8 (1); for grades 9-12 (2); for adults (3).

Beck, Henry Charlton, ed. *A New Jersey Reader*. New Brunswick, New Jersey: Rutgers University Press, 1961. (2, 3)

An entertaining collection of stories and articles about New Jersey people, places, and events, both real and fictional, from Revolutionary times to the present by Andrew D. Mellick, Jr., Frank R. Stockton, Fletcher Pratt, Owen Johnson, Alexander Woollcott, John Brooks, Stephen Crane, J. C. Furnas, and others.

Beck, Henry Charlton. *The Roads of Home: Lanes and Legends of New Jersey.* Foreword by Carl Carmer. New Brunswick, New Jersey: Rutgers University Press, 1956. (2, 3)

A chatty, rambling blend of "book-say with folksay," giving many sidelights on the history of many parts of the state.

Beers, Lorna. *Crystal Cornerstone.* New York: Harper and Brothers, 1933. (2)

Sixteen-year-old Thaddeus decides not to go to the new college at Prince Towne, but to fight in the Revolution.

Bell, Kensil, *Jersey Rebel.* New York: Dodd, Mead and Company, 1951. (1, 2)

——. *Secret Mission for Valley Forge.* New York: Dodd, Mead and Company, 1955. (1, 2)

Adventures of a teen-ager as spy for General Washington in South Jersey.

Bleeker, Sonia. *Delaware Indians: Eastern Fishermen and Farmers.* New York: William Morrow and Company, 1953. (1)

An illustrated factual account of the mode of life of the tribe which included the Lenape of New Jersey.

Cawley, James S. and Margaret. *Exploring the Little Rivers of New Jersey.* New Brunswick, New Jersey: Rutgers University Press, 1961. Originally published by the Princeton University Press, 1942. (2, 3)

Maps and 77 photographs, plus text that imparts the peculiar qualities of each river, make this an invaluable guide to exploration by land or water in the state.

Crowell, Victor L. *The Wonderful World of New Jersey: Our Natural Resources.* New Brunswick, New Jersey: Rutgers University Press, 1955. (1, 2, 3)
Written for use in school, this closely packed, authoritative account of the water, soil, animal, and mineral resources and their conservation is useful to students and adults alike. Illustrated with many fine photographs.

Cunningham, John T. *Garden State: The Story of Agriculture in New Jersey.* New Brunswick, New Jersey: Rutgers University Press, 1955. (2, 3)
———. *Made in New Jersey: The Industrial Story of a State.* New Brunswick, New Jersey: Rutgers University Press, 1954. (2, 3)
———. *The New Jersey Shore.* Maps by William N. Canfield. New Brunswick, New Jersey: Rutgers University Press, 1958. (2, 3)
———. *This is New Jersey: From High Point to Cape May.* Maps by William N. Canfield. New Brunswick, New Jersey: Rutgers University Press, 1953. (1, 2, 3)
An invaluable set, profusely illustrated with photographs, covering many aspects of the state's history and development.

Curtis, Alice T. *Little Maid of Monmouth.* New York: Alfred A. Knopf, 1953. (1)
Adventures of a little girl who lived near Monmouth Court House in 1778.

De Angeli, Marguerite. *Jared's Island.* New York: Doubleday and Company, 1947. (1)
Treasure-hunting on the Jersey Coast in the 1760's.

Dorian, Edith. *High-Water Cargo*. New York: McGraw-Hill Book Company, 1950. (1, 2)

An exciting adventure story set in New Brunswick during the era of canal traffic.

Duncan, John M. *Twelve Days 'til Trenton*. New York: McGraw-Hill Book Company, 1958. (2)

Matt Doliber, from Massachusetts, and Brad, a Virginian, become friends in the Continental Army and, at the Battle of Trenton, keep each other from deserting.

Faden, William. *The Province of New Jersey, Divided into East and West,* Commonly Called The Jerseys. [New Jersey Historical Society, 1960.] (1, 2, 3)

Facsimile of a famous 1778 map, printed in six colors on fine hand-made paper from plates prepared for this edition in Italy.

Ford, Paul L. *Janice Meredith*. New York: Dodd, Mead and Company, 1899. (2, 3)

A novel dating from the era in which Stockton wrote, of romance in the Raritan Valley during the Revolution.

Gale, Elizabeth. *Katrina Van Ost and the Silver Rose*. New York: G. P. Putnam's Sons, 1924. (1)

Twelve-year-old Katrina, orphaned in Holland, comes to live with a cousin on the " Hackensacky " River.

Hackett, James P. *The New Jersey Citizen*. New Brunswick, New Jersey: Rutgers University Press, 1957. (2, 3)

Clear and informative chapters on every aspect of the state government, including a brief review of the state's history.

Hagaman, Adaline P. *The Story of New Jersey*. Enl. ed. Lincoln, Nebraska: University Publishing Company, 1957. (1)

More simply written than O'Connell and strictly a textbook; covers history through the Revolution in some detail with brief chapters on the period following, and on "Using Nature's gifts wisely."

Kraft, Bayard R. *Under Barnegat's Beam*. New York: Appleton, Parsons and Company, 1960. (2, 3)

Life and lore of the Jersey shore in readable style and with many photographs.

Meader, Stephen. *Fish Hawk's Nest*. New York: Harcourt, Brace and Company, 1952. (1, 2)
Story of smuggling at Cape May in 1820.

Mellick, Andrew D. *Lesser Crossroads*. Ed. by Hubert G. Schmidt from *The Story of an Old Farm*. New Brunswick, New Jersey: Rutgers University Press, 1948. (2, 3)

Account of a middle-class German family, the Moelichs, who settled in Somerset County in 1751, which provides much background for the Revolutionary era.

New Jersey. *Manual of the New Jersey Legislature, 1872 to date*. J. Joseph Gribbins, Editor and Publisher, 589 Bellevue Avenue, Trenton, New Jersey. Annual. (1, 2, 3)

Among other data, provides a history of New Jersey; a list of Governors, 1624 to date; information on the state seal, flower, etc.; and a list of East and West Jersey Proprietors.

O'Connell, Margaret. *Jersey's Story*. Chicago, Illinois: Lyons and Carnahan, 1958. (1, 2)

Copiously illustrated with photographs by the author, this text for upper grades tells the story through the Civil War and provides also a number of useful lists, such as " Famous Firsts," " Famous Jerseyites," and " How some towns received their names."

Peare, Catherine O. *John Woolman, Child of Light*. New York: Vanguard Press, 1954. (1, 2)

Life story of the American Quaker, one of the first to fight against slavery.

Pierce, Arthur D. *Iron in the Pines: The Story of New Jersey's Ghost Towns and Bog Iron*. New Brunswick, New Jersey: Rutgers University Press, 1957. (2, 3)

Valuable account of this early industry and of the history of South Jersey—the " Wharton Estate," Martha and Etna Furnaces, and the ghost town of Batsto.

——. *Smugglers' Woods: Jaunts and Journeys in Colonial and Revolutionary New Jersey*. New Brunswick, New Jersey: Rutgers University Press, 1960. (2, 3)

Excellent account of the " cold war " before and during the Revolution, the economic and maritime contribution of the state to the winning of the war, as well as the story of Captain Huddy and the Tea-Burning.

Sherman, Edith B. *Mistress Madcap*. New York: Doubleday and Company, 1935. (1, 2)

Two teen-age girls living in Newark and their part in the Revolution.

Sterne, Emma G. *Drums of Monmouth.* New York:
Dodd, Mead and Company, 1935. (1, 2)
Story of Philip Freneau, poet of the Revolution.

Stockton, Frank R. *Stories of New Jersey.* New Brunswick, New Jersey: Rutgers University Press, 1961.
(1, 2, 3)
Reissue of a minor classic of local history, presenting
stories from the earliest settlers to the Mexican War
period. First published in 1896.

Taylor, David. *Lights Across the Delaware.* Philadelphia: J. B. Lippincott Company, 1954. (2, 3)
A lively tale of Phoebe, ardent patriot, and her Quaker
sweetheart and their involvement in the preparations for
the crossing of the Delaware.

Tyler, David B. *The Bay & River, Delaware: A Picto-
rial History.* Cambridge, Maryland: Cornell Maritime
Press, 1955. (2, 3)
Designed to present in many pictures and in text the
close relationship of the peoples and states of the Delaware Valley; emphasizes maritime and naval activities,
such as the War with the Barbary Pirates, the exploits
of Captain Barry, and the shipbuilding industry.

Wibberley, Leonard. *John Barry, Father of the Navy.*
Ariel Books. New York: Farrar, Straus, 1957. (2)
Biography of a great naval hero of the Revolution.

Wildes, Harry Emerson. *Delaware.* Rivers of America
Series. New York: Farrar and Rinehart, 1940. (2, 3)
Emphasizes changes along the shores of this great river
from colonial settlement to the twentieth century.

Wildes, Harry Emerson. *Twin Rivers: The Raritan and the Passaic*. Rivers of America Series. New York: Farrar and Rinehart, 1943. (2, 3)

Story of the heartland of the state in colonial and revolutionary times and during the industrial revolution.

Writers' Project. *New Jersey: A Guide to Its Present and Past*. Rev. ed. American Guide Series. New York: Hastings House, 1959. (2, 3)

A general view of the state, describing its cities, towns, and tours; a photographic reproduction of the 1939 edition.